HERITAGE LANDSCAPES

Editor
Donna Wood

Designer
Andrew Milne

Picture Researcher
Alice Earle

Image retouching and internal repro
Jacqueline Street

Cartography provided by the Mapping Services Department of AA Publishing

Production
Rachel Davis

Produced by AA Publishing

ISBN: 978-0-7495-7076-7
and 978-0-7495-7121-4 (SS)

Published by AA Publishing (a trading name of AA Media Limited, whose registered office is Fanum House, Basing View, Basingstoke RG21 4EA; registered number 06112600).

A04505

Printed in China by 1010 Printing International Ltd

theAA.com/shop

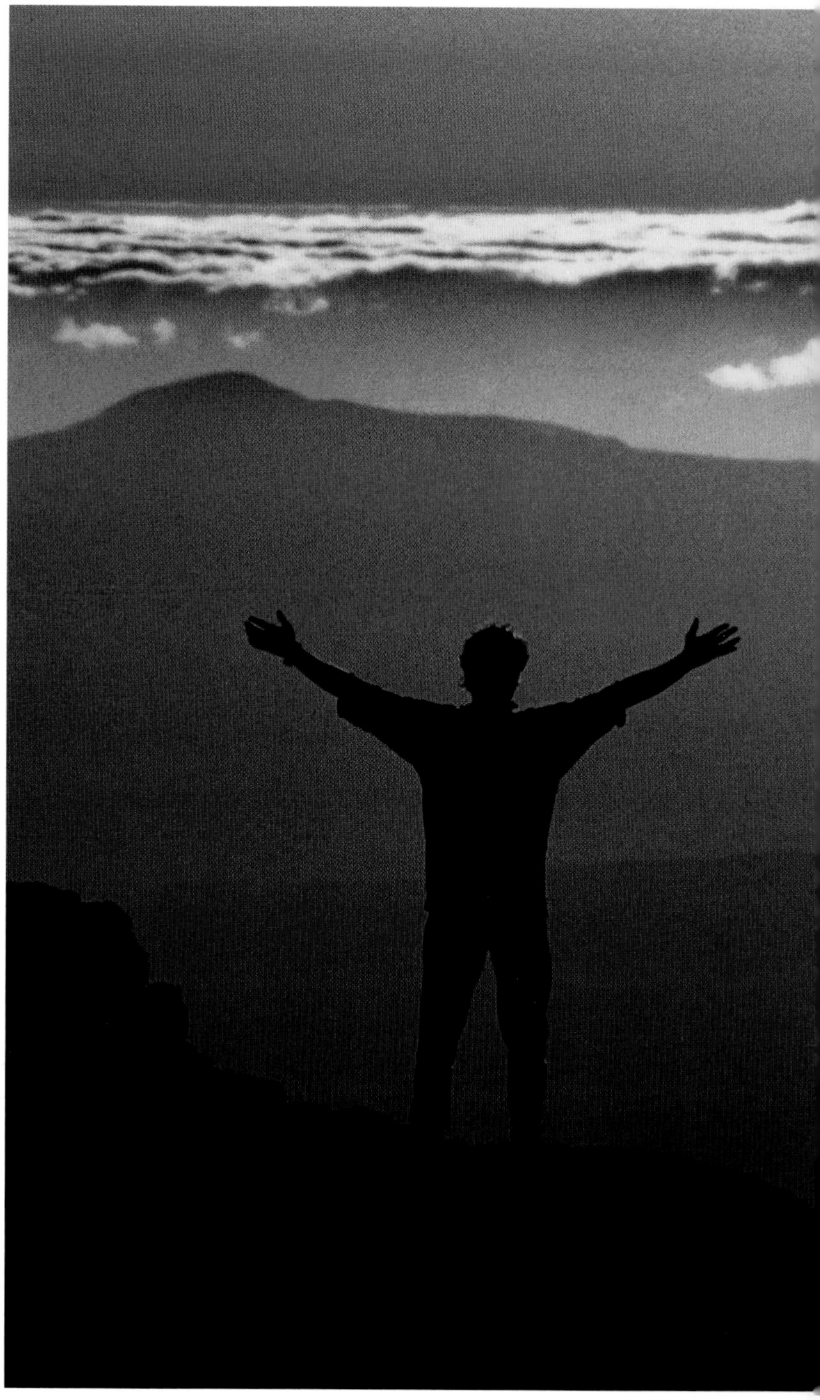

Author's Dedication
To Amy, Chloe and Holly, granddaughters of Outstanding Natural Beauty

HERITAGE LANDSCAPES

A guide to Britain's **Areas of Outstanding Natural Beauty**

ROLY SMITH

Contents / Locator Map

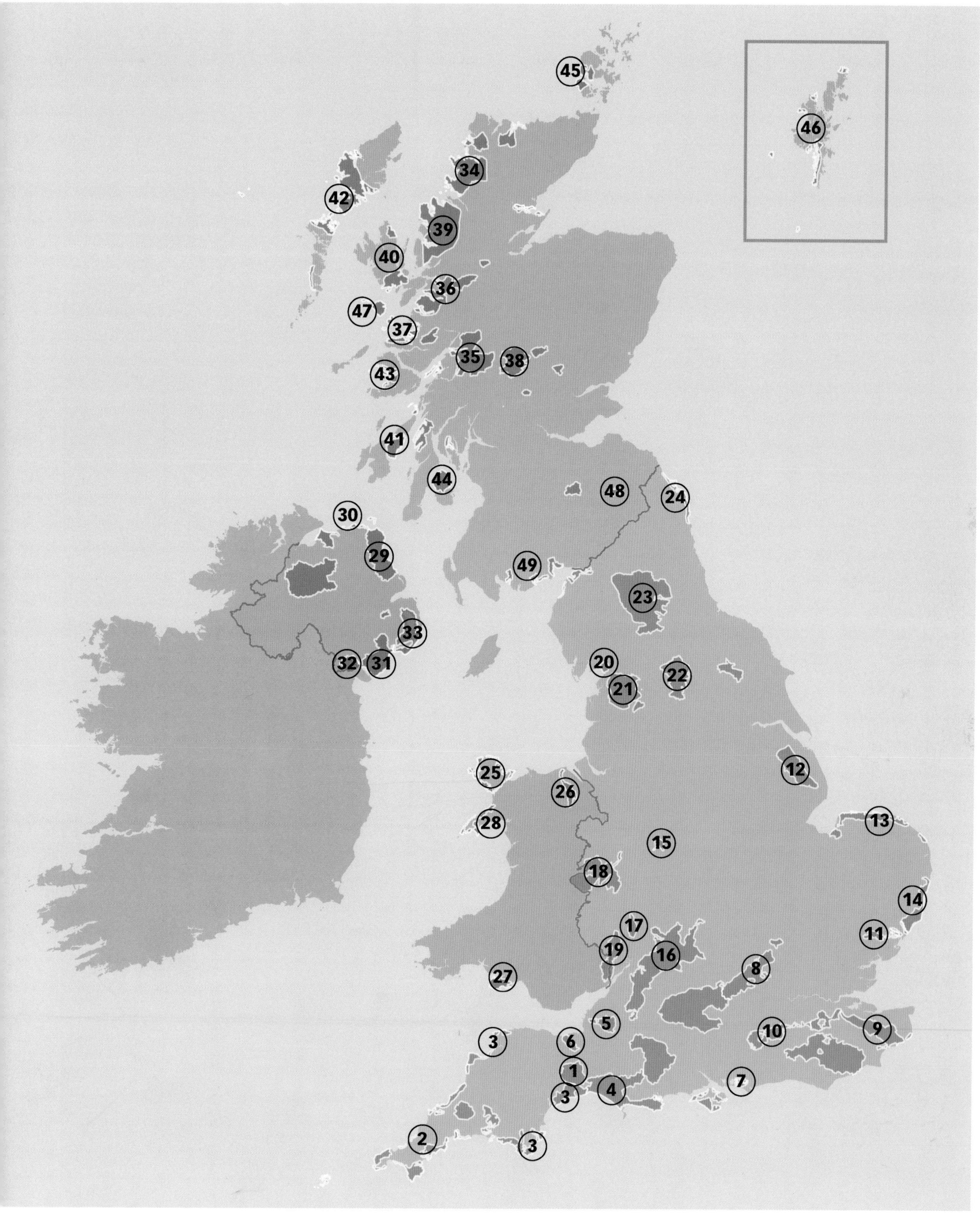

FOREWORD **MATT BAKER**

I have to be honest and say I never realized how much I appreciated our British landscape until I was 21 years old and standing outside a high street flat, two miles from London's Shepherd's Bush. It was here that I planned to stay while I was working on *Blue Peter*. Up until then, our sheep farm on the edge of the rugged Durham Dales had been nothing spectacular, just home.

As I began to realize how much the northern valleys steeped in a history of grazing meant to me, I lasted just six months in London before venturing towards greener pastures in search of trees and fields, and settled in the Chiltern Hills with my Dales-born sheepdog sidekick, Meg.

I've been lucky enough through *Countryfile, Secret Britain, Nature of Britain* and *Open Country* to have explored in depth all of the areas featured in this book. I've cycled and sailed, climbed and caved, hung and hang-glided, rambled and roamed all over the British Isles. It still amazes me that today, due to Britain's geological past, we are able to explore such a diverse collection of landscapes, from the rolling downs and chalk cliffs of Sussex to the dramatic shards of rock on the west coast of Scotland, all without stepping off our island.

I indulge in the thought that so many have trodden the paths before us, leaving a lasting legacy on the landscape. No matter what mark is imprinted, our nature and wildlife always seem to recover. I have always loved the Scottish border country. The thought of the battles that went on there has intrigued me ever since I was a boy, and I would often stop my car as I drove up to college in Edinburgh and imagine those bloodthirsty scenes echoing through the countryside around me.

On the face of it, we may well have a quaint piece of land, but I believe we have the benefit of at least four times that amount of landscape, as with every season our views change. How much more do we appreciate the sunshine as we amble down a country lane when we think back to the time we couldn't get the car along that same icy, sludgy stretch only six months earlier?

Having travelled the world, I can safely say that nowhere can match our eclectic mix of scenery. From shore to shore, our patchwork countryside, lovingly tended by farmers, the custodians of the land, is a joy to survey.

This beautiful book will take you around Britain, enlighten you to things you never knew and hopefully inspire you to visit the places you have never been to. For me, the most relaxing thing about spending time outdoors is adopting the slow pace of nature. You cannot rush it, so if you cannot beat it, join it.

I hope you enjoy this book at a leisurely pace and – using an analogy I try to apply to my life in general – always stop and appreciate the flowers instead of rushing straight for the gate.

Opposite The green sheep-farming lands of the northern valleys, where Matt was brought up
Above Matt with his sheepdog, Meg

INTRODUCTION

CINDERELLA LANDSCAPES

'AONBs? What are they?' asked a friend who I'd thought was quite environmentally aware. When I described the honey-stoned Cotswolds, the glorious, castle-studded Northumberland coast and the seabird-haunted cliffs of Cornwall, he responded, 'Oh yes, I've heard of them.' That's always been the trouble with Areas of Outstanding Natural Beauty – we all know *where* they are but – and it has much to do with that clumsy, bureaucratic title – few people know *what* they are.

Although they were set up 60 years ago under the 1949 National Parks and Access to the Countryside Act, the same ground-breaking legislation that established our well-known and beloved national parks, the AONBs of England, Wales and Northern Ireland, and the NSAs (National Scenic Areas), their equivalents in Scotland, have always been regarded as the Cinderellas among British landscapes. The situation has even led some unkind critics to modify the awful acronym to Any Other Nice Bits or, even more cruelly, Another Officially Named Bureaucracy.

No less a Prince Charming than Professor Adrian Phillips, former Director of the Countryside Commission, former chairman of the Commission on Protected Areas of the International Union for Conservation of Nature (IUCN) and board member of the Cotswolds Conservation Board, confessed to the Cinderella tag that AONBs suffer in a speech celebrating the 60th anniversary of the 1949 Act.

'The 1949 Act appeared to accord a second-class status to AONBs,' he said. 'Bearing in mind the strategic importance of many of the AONB landscapes, and that overall the AONBs cover roughly twice the area of the (national) parks in England, it would seem that the AONBs were the Cinderellas of the protected landscapes family.'

Cotswold beauty (below)
Ivy-clad houses of honey-coloured stone line the High Street at Burford

Northumberland gem (right)
The Northumberland coast at Dunstanburgh with the castle on the horizon

AONBs came to be recognized solely as areas meriting special landscape protection...

Varied landscapes

The designation process for AONBs had been similar to that for national parks but, under the 1949 Act, the way in which AONBs were to be run was largely left to the discretion of local authorities, and no funds were made available for their protection.

Phillips said that while the Act was a milestone in British conservation history, the benefit of hindsight revealed major shortcomings. It split, for example, nature conservation from landscape protection and its enjoyment, and focused only on the 'best' landscapes, largely ignoring the rest. 'It also created a tension between landscape conservation and recreation in national parks, and left AONBs as second-class protected landscapes – both issues that it took many years to resolve.' Many would say that these issues have still not been resolved.

But Phillips insisted that the landscapes of the AONBs were much more varied than those of the national parks, citing as examples the granite archipelago of Scilly, the high moors of the North Pennines, the chalk hills of southeast England, the coastlines of the Solway, Northumberland, Dorset, Devon and Cornwall – and much else besides.

Indeed, in recent years, several AONBs and NSAs have made the step up and been granted full national park status. Examples are the South Hampshire Coast, which was subsumed into the New Forest National Park when it was established in 2005, and East Hampshire and the rolling Sussex Downs, which became the South Downs National Park in 2010. Across the border, the NSAs of Loch Lomond and the Trossachs became Scotland's first national park in 2002, followed a year later by the rugged, semi-arctic Cairngorms.

What are AONBs and NSAs?

Under the 1949 Act, AONBs were acknowledged to have exactly the same kind of landscape qualities as national parks, but to be of a 'second order' of importance, which did not require the same intensity of planning control as the parks or National Nature Reserves (NNRs). Originally described as 'conservation areas', they were to be administered by local authorities with similar, though more flexible, conservation policies as national parks. Even at this early stage, it was proposed that they should have the principle of the protection of natural beauty above that of open-air enjoyment.

In the event, however, AONBs came to be recognized solely as areas meriting special landscape protection, and their administration was left to the whim of the individual local authorities within which they fell. Earlier ideas for each having specially appointed advisory committees were abandoned, along with any reference to their scientific interest or recreational value as reasons for designation.

The first AONB to be designated, on 10 December 1956, was the Gower, but it was chosen not for its classic Carboniferous limestone coastline and wonderful heathland environment, but because it was the last outpost of unspoilt natural beauty in industrial South Wales. Much the same reason had been given for the designation of the Peak District as the first national park five years before, which occupied a similar position in northern England.

In Scotland, the 40 NSAs were designated by the Secretary of State for Scotland under the 1972 Town and Country Planning Act in 1980 and 1981. This followed the publication in 1978 of the seminal report entitled *Scotland's Scenic Heritage* by the Countryside Commission for Scotland (now Scottish Natural Heritage). Northern Ireland's AONBs were set up by the Department of the Environment for Northern Ireland under the provisions of the Nature Conservation and Amenity Lands (Northern Ireland) Order of 1985.

Varied landscapes Unspoilt natural beauty at Peninnis Head on the Isles of Scilly (top), the high moors of the North Pennines (centre), and sunrise at Cley next the Sea windmill, Norfolk (bottom)

Designation of AONBs and NSAs

Natural England (NE), the Countryside Council for Wales (CCW), the Department of the Environment for Northern Ireland and Scottish Natural Heritage (SNH) are the bodies responsible for formally designating AONBs and NSAs, and for advising on policies for their protection.

These agencies act as national watchdogs over the areas, ensuring that they are properly conserved and enhanced. As with the national parks, designation nowadays also recognizes the needs of the local community and economy, while seeking to protect and enhance natural beauty. In addition to landscape conservation, measures include the protection of flora, fauna and geological features, and the conservation of archaeological, architectural and other vernacular features.

The responsibility of care of AONBs and NSAs is assumed by local authorities and the rural community, providing a context for what is described as 'low-key, long-term action', relying on partnership with local people. As a result of this local bias, the planning and management approach of individual AONBs or NSAs can vary considerably, especially as most AONBs fall within the areas of more than one local authority.

To encourage consistent policies and positive coordination, all the AONBs in England, Wales and Northern Ireland have undertaken the following actions, while SNH follows similar policies north of the border:

- The formation of Joint Advisory Committees or similar bodies. These comprise representatives not only of the different local authorities, but also of local landowners, farmers, residents and conservation and recreation interests.
- The appointment of AONB officers to coordinate local management operations.
- The preparation of Statements of Intent (or Commitment) and Management Plans.

Precious woodland (above)
Help is offered to farmers and landowners in AONBs to encourage landscape conservation and to preserve natural features such as bluebells and other wild flowers

Small tortoiseshell butterfly on lavender flower (right)

Raising awareness

Help is offered to farmers and landowners in AONBs and NSAs to encourage vital landscape conservation. For example, advice and grants can save hedgerows, wildflower meadows and woodland, and discourage the draining and ploughing up of ancient flower-rich pastures.

Grants for safeguarding traditional farmed landscapes in a number of AONBs and NSAs are available through schemes run by the Department for Environment, Food and Rural Affairs (Defra), the Northern Ireland Environment Agency, the Welsh Assembly Government and the Scottish Government. These grant schemes reduce the financial pressures on farmers, which in the past have led them to remove traditional landscape features in the interests of greater efficiency.

The National Association for Areas of Outstanding Natural Beauty (NAAONB) was formed in 1998 as an independent organization to act on behalf of the AONBs in England, Wales and Northern Ireland. There is no similar organization in Scotland. By raising awareness of the importance of AONBs among local communities, local authorities and visitors, it seeks to foster a commitment to the AONBs, encourage local partnerships and generate informed support from visitors.

The NAAONB also recognizes that managing visitor numbers is a growing challenge. Control measures to avoid damage – ranging from parking restrictions to steering people away from the most sensitive sites – are only part of the answer. The provision of leaflets, trails and ranger services within the AONBs can help to show visitors why the landscape is precious and how to protect, as well as quietly enjoy, its fragile natural beauty.

The future

The long-term vision of the NAAONB is to be part of a major national independent body representing those responsible for and involved in the management of all protected landscapes in the UK. It also seeks to work closely with Natural England and the Countryside Council for Wales to realize the opportunities presented by current legislation, such as the Countryside and Rights of Way Act of 2000, also popularly known as the Right to Roam.

But starting as it does from a very low base when it comes to identity, everything will depend on a number of imponderable issues. These include the future support of those government agencies, which are smarting from severe budgetary restrictions, to continue to designate and watch over these precious, if often unregarded, landscapes. However, in April 2011, country lovers were encouraged to hear an announcement from the Coalition Government that Defra would be taking over the direct funding of AONBs through a new agreement between itself, Natural England and the NAAONB. Claiming 'a new era for AONBs', Environment Minister Richard Benyon said: 'We need AONBs to ensure that our most important and treasured landscapes continue to thrive and are enjoyed by future generations. They are crucial to our environmental objectives.'

So maybe these beautiful Cinderellas will, at last, be invited to the ball.

... So maybe these beautiful Cinderellas will, at last, be invited to the ball

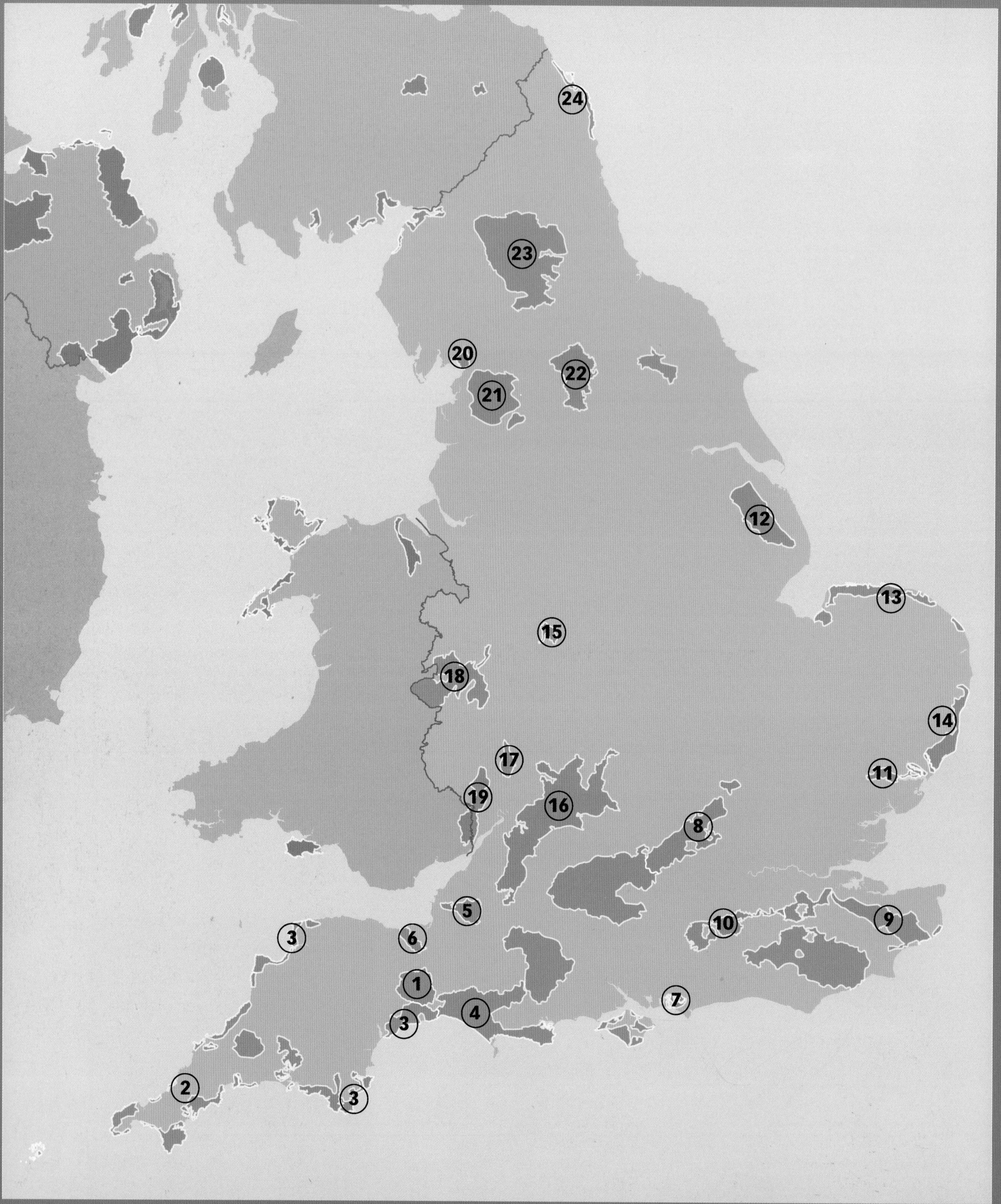

24
23
20
22
21
12
13
15
18
14
17
11
19
16
8
5
10
9
3
6
1
7
4
3
2
3

ENGLAND

1

2

3

1 Rippling shingle patterns at Holkham Bay on the Norfolk Coast **2** 'Tramlines' in a wheat field at Wenlock Edge, Shropshire Hills **3** Waterfall at Bowlees, North Pennines

BLACKDOWN HILLS

Motorists speeding south on the M5 motorway as it threads through the Vale of Taunton may notice the steep, heavily wooded northern escarpment of the Blackdown Hills over to the east.

Straddling the borders of Devon and Somerset, the geology of the Blackdown Hills is unique in the West Country, as it is founded on the only extensive outcrop of Upper Greensand in the region. This fact accounts for the region's distinctive topography and also for its unusual flora, which thrives on the rare non-calcareous greensand, and its distinctive cob-built vernacular buildings.

The northern escarpment, which rises to a height of 1,035ft (315m) at Staple Hill, slopes gently to the south as a plateau, deeply dissected by southward-running valleys, such as those of the main rivers: the Tale, Otter and Yarty. The only exception to this generally southward drainage pattern is the valley of the Culm, which runs westwards to join the Exe to the north of Exeter.

The best examples of the natural landscape and wildlife of the Blackdown Hills can be found at the nature reserves of Ashculm Turbary and Lickham Common, with their distinctive unimproved acid-loving vegetation that favours the Upper Greensand.

'Turbary' is the word used to describe an area where turves of peat were formerly cut for fuel. At Ashculm Turbary, a range of habitats exists, from the acid bog (from which the turves were cut) to birch scrub and wet alder and willow carr. Up to 40 different species of bird have been recorded here. The 10-acre Lickham Common reserve still has large areas dominated by purple moor grass and oak woodland in the drier areas, and bog myrtle and alder and alder buckthorn in the wetter spots.

Chertstone villages

Up on the exposed plateau, away from the northern escarpment, which rises to a height of nearly 1,000ft (300m), the situation is open and windswept, and sheep farming predominates. Skylarks trill on their silver spirals of sound, and the views extend for miles over Devon to the distant blue heights of Dartmoor; to Somerset across to the Brendon Hills and beyond, over the M5 and Vale of Taunton; and south, towards the glittering waters of Lyme Bay.

Lower down in the wooded valleys, small villages such as Churchinford, Stockland and Dunkeswell have grown up in the time-honoured English way, surrounded by an intricate network of high-hedged lanes and small, irregular fields with, probably, prehistoric origins. Many of these villages have been built with the

1 An aerial view of the Hembury Hill Iron Age hillfort **2** Goldfinch perched on burdock seeds **3** A bank vole peeps out from a dry-stone wall

2

3

1

2

unique local building stone known as chertstone. Together with the cob and thatch of the cottages of the smaller hamlets and farms, this adds to the highly distinctive identity of the region.

Cob is an ancient and versatile building material, used to build houses since prehistoric times, particularly in places where wood or stone was difficult to obtain. It consists of a mixture of clay, sand, straw and water, and is both inexpensive to make and virtually fireproof. In the UK, it is most strongly associated with the counties of Devon and Cornwall. The traditional thatched roofs of older cottages would originally have been made from local heather harvested on the moorland heights of the Blackdowns. Today, however, reed brought in from Norfolk is generally used.

Cross-country highway

Early man obviously found the heights of the Blackdown Hills to his liking. The great double-ditched Iron Age hillfort of Hembury, overlooking the A373 and the little, bustling market town of Honiton, is perhaps the finest in Devon and commands a spectacular view across the South Devon countryside. At an impressive 885ft (270m), the highest part of the 7-acre, pear-shaped Hembury Fort is known as the Trundle, and was first occupied some 5,000 years ago by a Neolithic causewayed camp. Half of the fort was later reused by the invading Romans, who built a military fort here to command the Fosse Way, their important cross-country highway linking Leicester and Exeter.

A much more recent landmark in the north of the area is the Wellington Monument on Wellington Hill, 2 miles (3.2km) south of the Somerset town of Wellington. It was erected on land belonging to the Duke of Wellington, to celebrate his victory at the Battle of Waterloo in 1815. The foundation stone was laid two years later, although the monument was not completed until 1854. Inspired by an Egyptian obelisk, its design is also said to resemble the bayonets used by Wellington's victorious troops. The monument is owned by the National Trust, and is sometimes floodlit at night.

Although there are no large towns within the 143 square miles (370sq km) of the AONB, which was designated in 1990, Honiton, just outside the designation, is the most important service centre. The original town at Honiton was twice destroyed by fire in 1747 and 1765, but it was rebuilt in the handsome, late Georgian style. Famous in the past for its lacemaking – Queen Victoria's wedding veil and part of her dress was made of Honiton lace (see box) – the town was also a centre for glovemaking. It still holds an annual fair, which was first recorded in 1257, in July.

The lasting impression of the Blackdown Hills is of a soft, archetypal English landscape of high-hedged fields, grazed by black-and-white Friesian dairy cows, and well-wooded valleys, leading up to the breezy heights of the open Blackdown plateau.

1 The wren is a common bird in the Blackdown Hills **2** An inviting path through the woods of Hembury Hill **3** A typical thatched Devon longhouse near Honiton **4** The Wellington Monument **5** An example of delicate Honiton lace

3

4

5

HONITON LACE

Honiton's bobbin lace industry is thought to have been founded by Flemish refugees escaping from persecution during the late 16th century. Interestingly, names of Flemish origin still occur in local surnames.

Although known as Honiton lace, it was actually made in the surrounding villages and marketed in the town. Making the lace was a team effort, with specialist lace-makers who used pairs of the slender, pointed bobbins unique to Honiton to create the floral motifs known as sprigs, while others would stitch them together to make larger pieces. Royalty, such as Charles I in the 17th century, helped to make the lace fashionable and sought-after.

Allhallows Museum in Honiton High Street has one of the most comprehensive collections of Honiton lace in the world, including exquisite examples from the 16th to the early 20th centuries (left).

2

3

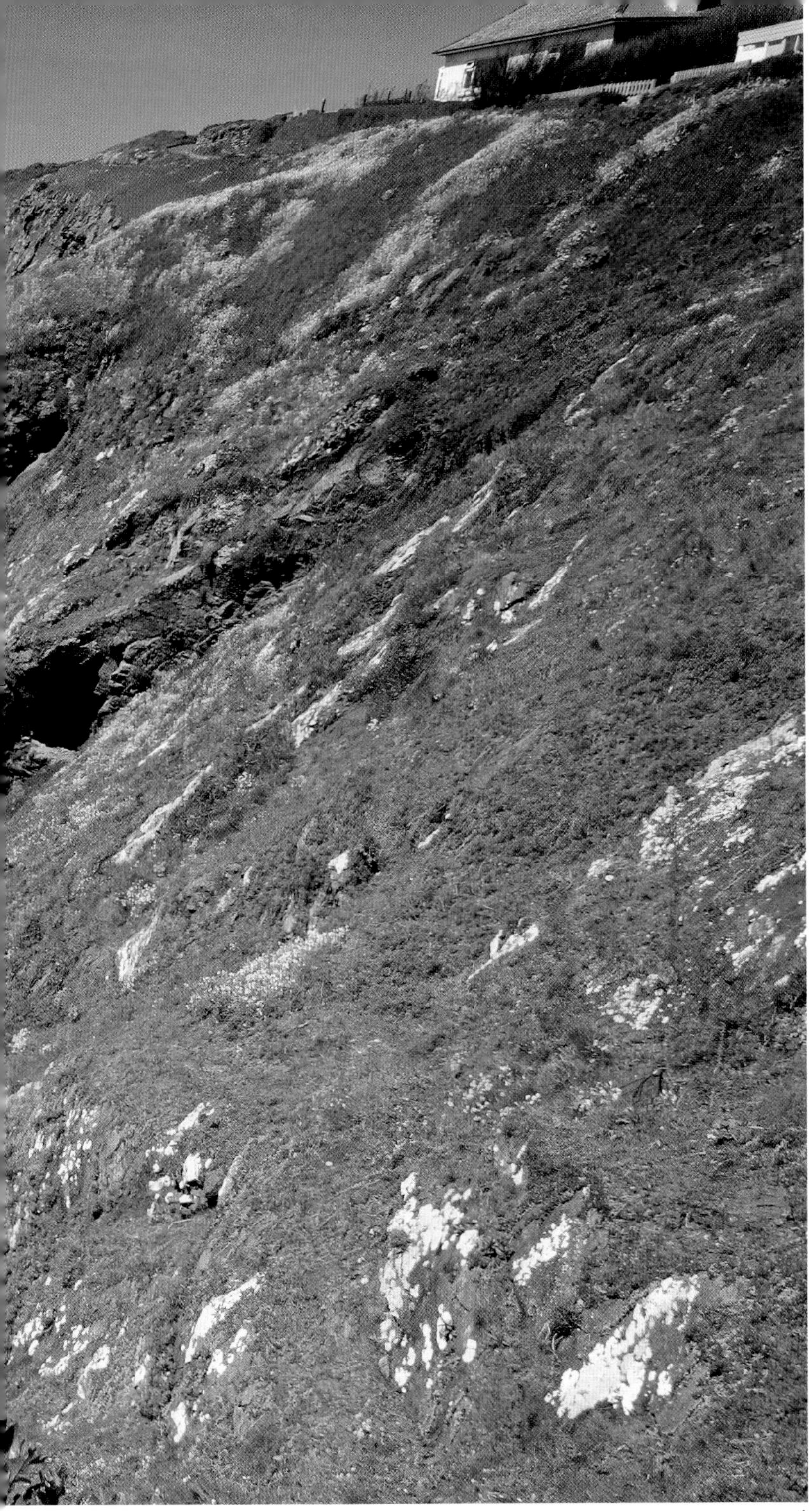

1

4

CORNWALL

Some of Britain's finest coastal scenery, from the rugged headlands of North Devon through to Land's End and the Lizard, together with the inland granite boss of Bodmin Moor, is included in this 370 square mile (958sq km) AONB.

Cornwall is one of Britain's most popular holiday destinations, with places like Land's End, the Lizard, St Michael's Mount, Looe and Polperro usually thronged with visitors during the summer season. Most holidaymakers, though, do not realize that much of the county is an AONB, specially protected to ensure Cornwall's long-term conservation so that future generations will also be able to enjoy its stunning beauty.

Designated in 1959, the Cornwall AONB is one of the most fragmented of all the British AONBs. A total of 146 miles (235km) of its coast is also designated as Heritage Coast, and the area around West Penwith is classified as an Environmentally Sensitive Area. The South West Coast Path, the 613-mile (987km) National Trail that rounds the southwestern tip of Britain, follows a rollercoaster route around the Cornish peninsula.

The most northerly point of the Cornwall AONB is the Hartland section, north of Bude, which includes the rugged headlands and bays of Sharpnose Point, near Morwenstow. South of the surfers' paradise of Bude Bay, the AONB includes the sands of Widemouth Bay and continues south to Pentire Point, passing Tintagel Head with its ruined castle, the legendary capital of King Arthur, and Boscastle, with its narrow, fjord-like harbour.

Moving west, the next section takes in Trevose Head, with its gleaming white lighthouse and the steeply winding, wooded valley of the Camel estuary towards Wadebridge, covering 9.6 square miles (25sq km) and including the popular town of Padstow. The area around the tourist honeypot of Newquay is excluded, but the AONB boundary takes in the resort of Perranporth, or Piran's Port (St Piran is the patron saint of Cornwall), and the headland of St Agnes, with its ancient beacon standing on a fine viewpoint just inland at 620ft (190m) above the sea.

The cliffs of Portreath are highlights of the next section and lead down to Godrevy Point, overlooking St Ives Bay. Most of the rocky Penwith peninsula is included, with its interesting remains of tin and copper mines (see box, page 22) along the coast and around the village of St Just. Land's End is one of Britain's most famous landmarks, where every year over a million visitors watch the Atlantic breakers smash on the westernmost point of England.

1 The rugged cliffs around Lizard Point **2** Coast-loving sea thrift growing on the cliffs near Gunwalloe **3** Droskyn sundial and the wide sands of Perran beach **4** Boats moored in Coverack harbour on the Lizard peninsula

Turning east, the romantic granite island of St Michael's Mount, reached by a causeway only at low tide, overlooks its bay as a prelude to the rugged heathlands of Goonhilly Downs and the Lizard peninsula, a geological National Nature Reserve (NNR) that marks the southernmost tip of Britain. The peninsula is the best-preserved example in Britain of an exposed ophiolite, a geological formation that represents a section of the oceanic crust thrust onto the continental crust.

It is a strange coincidence that much of the Lizard peninsula is composed of a greenish rock called serpentine, which resembles the skin of the reptile. The name Lizard may be a corruption of the Cornish *Lys Ardh*, meaning 'high court', but its original name was the Celtic *Predannack*, meaning 'the British one', and during the Bronze Age, when the Cornish tin trade first started, Britain was known in Greek as 'Pretannike'. The Lizard lighthouse was built at Lizard Point in 1752, and the Lizard lifeboat station, operated by the RNLI, is situated at Kilcobben Cove.

The area around the Fal estuary is one of Europe's best examples of a ria (drowned estuary). The AONB takes in the sheltered bays and patchwork-quilt landscape on this southern coastline of the county, sometimes known as the Cornish Riviera or the Roseland, up to St Austell and including Mevagissey.

The last two sections of the Cornwall AONB include Gribbin Head, Fowey and Polperro, up to Looe, and the superb viewpoint of Rame Head, with its ruined 14th-century chapel dedicated to St Michael. Inland, the great granite boss of Bodmin Moor covers 80 square miles (208sq km) of the AONB and gives the appearance of Dartmoor in miniature, with wild, open moorland topped by rocky tors carved into sensuous shapes by the frost, wind and rain.

TIN MINING IN CORNWALL

We know that tin has been mined in Cornwall at least since the Bronze Age (between 2000 and 500 BC) because Phoenician traders from the eastern Mediterranean are known to have obtained the ore – an essential component in making bronze – from Cornwall during that time.

The Greek writer Diodorus Siculus describes tin mining in Britain in around 1st century BC and mentions an island called Ictis, to where tin in large quantities was brought in carts for export. Several locations have been suggested for Ictis, which means 'tin port', including St Michael's Mount.

For many centuries, Cornwall provided the UK's tin, copper and arsenic, originally found as alluvial deposits in the gravel of stream beds or as lodes outcropping on the cliffs.

The first underground mines were sunk as early as the 16th century, and the Cornish tin-mining industry continued into the mid-19th century.

1 The Towanroath engine house at the Wheal Coates tin mine, near Chapel Porth **2** View of the sea from Rosewall Hill, on the Land's End peninsula **3** The Cheesewring, a strange granite tor on Stowe's Hill overlooking the Cheesewring Quarry **4** Rusting footpath sign at St Keverne on the Lizard peninsula

1

2

3

4

DEVON: NORTH, SOUTH & EAST

Devon is not just famous for its cream teas. Some of the most spectacular scenery in Britain is found around its coast, which is covered by no fewer than three AONBs: the rocky coast of North Devon between Ilfracombe and Hartland; Britain's finest ria (drowned estuary) in South Devon, between Torbay and Plymouth; and the rich pastures and holiday honeypots of East Devon between Lyme Regis and Budleigh Salterton.

North Devon

Stretching west from Combe Martin to the Cornish border, the dramatic coastline of North Devon offers beetling cliffs and treacherous underwater reefs, as well as sandy dunes and beaches. Designated an AONB in 1959, the area covers 66 square miles (171sq km), including the Heritage Coasts of Hartland and North Devon, either side of Barnstaple and Bideford, and the tidal estuaries of the Rivers Torridge and Taw. The South West Coast Path National Trail traces one of its most spectacular sections along this length of the North Devon coast.

In the north of the AONB, steeply dipping rocks form an extension of the upland mass of neighbouring Exmoor, characterized by hog's-back cliffs around Combe Martin and Ilfracombe. The best known of these are the Great Hangman and Little Hangman (just outside the AONB) and Bull Point.

Further south, the great headlands of Morte Point and Baggy Point shelter the sandy expanses of Morte Bay and Braunton Burrows. Continuing south is the great open expanse of Barnstaple Bay, sometimes also known as Bideford Bay, which leads down to Westward Ho! Named after Charles Kingsley's adventure story about Elizabethan sailors, this is the only place in Britain with an exclamation mark in its name.

Braunton Burrows, a National Nature Reserve (NNR), is famous for its rare marsh orchids and unparalleled range of coastal dune habitats. Both Braunton Burrows and the Northam Burrows Country Park across the Taw estuary are also home to other rarities, such as glasswort, sea spurge and sea holly, as well as common blue and brown argus butterflies, ringed plovers, curlews, shelducks and oystercatchers.

From here, the AONB sweeps around picturesque cobble-streeted Clovelly to the towering headland of Hartland Point, known to Roman sailors as 'the Promontory of Hercules', and surely one of the most awe-inspiring places on the coastline

1 Vertically faulted and folded rock strata at Hartland Quay **2** The glorious sandy beach at Saunton Sands **3** Sea holly growing at Braunton Burrows **4** Clovelly's steeply cobbled street is popular with visitors and becomes very crowded in summer

2

3

4

of Britain. The 300ft (90m) high cliffs are seen at their dramatic best when being lashed by the frequent Atlantic gales. This is an elemental place, watched over by a coastguard station on the clifftop and with one of the strongest lighthouse beams in Britain situated halfway down the cliff.

The AONB also takes in the clifftop plateau inland from Hartland Point. This is scoured by deep valleys, which reach the coast as steep 'hanging' cliffs, down which great cascading waterfalls plunge straight into the waiting Atlantic. The remote cliffs and the grasslands on their tops are important ecological sites and include many Sites of Special Scientific Interest (SSSIs).

The North Devon AONB excludes the larger resorts of Ilfracombe, Bideford and Westward Ho! but includes a number of pretty fishing villages, such as Clovelly, Woolacombe, Bucks Mills and Croyde. About 12,000 people live in the North Devon AONB, with most of them employed in farming, fishing and the ever-increasing tide of tourism.

South Devon

Stretching along the coast from the holiday resort of Torbay to the great naval base at Plymouth, the South Devon AONB includes wild rocky headlands and cliffs as well as peaceful, secluded bays and wooded estuaries. It also contains some of the finest ria (drowned river valley) scenery in Britain, and the great winding, wooded estuaries of the Rivers Yealm, Erme, Avon and Dart, as well as the Salcombe–Kingsbridge estuary, which were submerged under rising sea levels after the last Ice Age.

Designated in 1959, the South Devon AONB covers 130 square miles (337sq km) and includes many SSSIs and 47 miles (75km) of the South Devon Heritage Coast, which is followed by the South West Coast Path.

The Field Studies Council has a famous National Nature Reserve at Slapton Ley, the largest freshwater lake in southwest England, where the 272-acre lake and reed beds provide valuable habitats for one of the widest ranges of birdlife in Britain. Over 230 species have been recorded in this sheltered lake, which is protected by a long shingle spit where, in winter, up to 10,000 gulls roost.

The waters beneath the rugged headlands of Bolt Head, Prawle Point (from the Old English for a lookout) and Start Point, where Precambrian rocks sweep down impressively to the sea, have been the graveyard for many ships over the years. The lighthouse at Start Point watches over the rocks where no fewer than five ships were wrecked during one night in 1891.

In sharp contrast, the Dart and the Salcombe–Kingsbridge estuaries are deeply wooded, with some lovely old oak woodlands offering tantalizing glimpses through the trees of the yacht-dotted

1

2

1 The Kingsbridge estuary seen from East Portlemouth **2** Richly textured shoreline rock at Rickham Sands, near Salcombe **3** Bird's foot trefoil growing at Start Point **4** Devon cream tea: scones smothered with clotted cream and strawberry jam

ANYONE FOR TEA?

The mouthwatering and cholesterol-raising traditional Devon cream tea (left) is said to have been invented by the monks of Tavistock Abbey in the 11th century. Apparently, the monks were the first to eat their bread with cream and jam, although tea, from China, didn't appear in England for hundreds of years.

The traditional Devon method of preparing a cream tea is to split the scones in two, cover each half with clotted cream, and then add strawberry jam on top. It is important that the scones are warm (ideally, freshly baked), that clotted (not whipped) cream is used, and that the jam is made from strawberries, although raspberry jam is occasionally used. Butter should never be spread on the scones, and the tea should be served with milk.

Across the Tamar in Cornwall, cream teas are traditionally served with a 'Cornish split' – a slightly sweet white bread roll – rather than a Devonian scone.

3

4

water beyond. Inland, the countryside of the South Hams is an area of mainly traditional Devon dairy farming, where those rich cream teas (see box, page 27) and delicious fudge originated.

This is truly deepest Devon, where flowering, deep-sunk hedgerows and ancient hollow lanes thread through the valleys. Thatched cottages, with their white-, pink- or ochre-painted wattle-and-daub walls, are the order of the day in the many small villages and hamlets.

The South Devon AONB population of about 33,000 is mainly concentrated in the larger settlements, such as Dartmouth, Wembury and Salcombe. Lively Dartmouth is an ancient sea-faring town on the western arm of the Dart estuary, and the home of the Britannia Royal Naval College, where future kings learned, and still learn, to sail as cadets. The bustling and attractive town itself reflects its history in its fine old buildings, such as the colonnaded Butterwalk, now housing a museum, which was built during the early 17th century.

The views from Wembury are dominated by the impressive whaleback of the Great Mewstone in Wembury Bay, an important nesting site for a range of seabirds. The former gunnery school of HMS *Cambridge* at Wembury Point, now in the hands of the National Trust, has reverted to a more peaceful purpose, encouraging important species, such as the cirl bunting, to breed.

Salcombe is a long-established haven for yachtsmen in one of the country's finest natural harbours – the Salcombe–Kingsbridge estuary – with its 2,000 acres of tidal creeks reaching far inland to Kingsbridge itself, the 'capital' of the South Hams district.

The AONB is popular with holidaymakers staying at the nearby resorts of Brixham, Paignton and Torquay, as well as with thousands of day-trippers from the city of Plymouth.

1

2

East Devon

East Devon has some of the richest pastures in England, making it ideal for raising Red Rubies, the russet-coated Devon breed of cattle. But it was the area's spectacular coastline that was behind its AONB designation in 1963.

Including most of the coast between Exmouth in the west and Lyme Regis to the east, the AONB covers 103 square miles (268sq km) and is home to the resorts of Budleigh Salterton, Sidmouth and Seaton, which make this stretch of coastline one of the most popular holiday destinations in Britain.

This AONB includes several attractive small towns and villages, among them Budleigh Salterton, once the home of the dashing Elizabethan adventurer Sir Walter Raleigh; Beer, with its traditional lobster fishing industry; and the charming village of Branscombe, on the coast between Sidmouth and Seaton, with its lovely cob and thatched cottages spreading up the steeply wooded slopes of a winding combe. The South West Coast Path follows the line of the clifftops.

The AONB coastline features the older Old Red Sandstone strata to the west, which ends near Budleigh Salterton, and the younger chalk cliffs to the east, which have their westernmost outcrop on the English Channel at Beer Head.

The estuaries, clifftop grasslands and wooded combes are important natural habitats, where seabirds swoop and cry, and other wildlife enjoys special protection. The most important of these sites is the NNR of the Undercliffs, a spectacular 5-mile (8km) landslip near Axmouth, designated for its geological and wildlife interest. The Axmouth–Lyme Undercliffs reserve covers 790 acres.

It was formed in geologically recent times – in 1839 – when a huge section of the chalk cliffs slumped towards the sea, creating a detached block known as Goat Island and a whole new diverse habitat of densely wooded cliffs and open slopes. This highly unstable and dangerous area is still slipping inexorably seawards, but rare flora such as the fen orchid, pendulous sedge and bog pimpernel and birds including the nightingale, stonechat and rock pipit are still to be found.

Inland, the landscape rises to high and, surprisingly, remote plateaus, sometimes topped by heathland and commons, especially in the west of the area. The East Devon plateau is split by rivers flowing down from the north, the most important of which are the Axe, the Sid, the Coly and the Otter. These wind down to the sea through a typically Devon landscape of high-hedged meadows reached by secluded, narrow lanes.

The East Devon AONB's population of about 15,000 has traditionally relied on fishing and farming, although tourism, with its associated service industries, is now becoming more important.

1 View of Sidmouth from the coastal path on Sidmouth Hill **2** The impression of an ammonite fossil on a Devon coastal cliff

DORSET

The unspoiled rural countryside of Thomas Hardy's Wessex novels can still be experienced in this 436 square mile (1,129sq km) AONB, which was designated in 1957. Covering nearly 40 per cent of Dorset, this AONB also takes in some fine coastlines, including the Purbeck Heritage Coast, which is a World Heritage Site and a holder of the Council of Europe's Nature Conservation Diploma.

Thomas Hardy was the pre-eminent novelist of the English naturalist movement. Born at Higher Bockhampton, where his cottage birthplace can still be visited, he based much of his work on his native Dorset, changing the names of the villages and towns in his novels. The essential flavour of these novels, such as *Far from the Madding Crowd* and *The Return of the Native*, can still be evoked in the area of the northern chalk ridge between Beaminster and the Axe Valley, eastwards to the Stour Valley near Blandford Forum. The southern arm of the Dorset Downs circles the town of Dorchester and reaches the coast at the Isle of Purbeck.

This is a countryside of broad, rolling downland with plenty of evidence of its prehistoric past. Not far from Dorchester (Hardy's Casterbridge, as in *The Mayor of Casterbridge*) is Maiden Castle, one of the finest Iron Age hillforts in Europe. Covering 46 acres, its massive ramparts, gateways and defences were finally overcome by the invading Romans under Vespasian in AD 43.

Chilling evidence of that invasion was found in a war cemetery just outside the main gate, where a Roman ballista bolt was discovered still lodged in the spine of a skeleton of a defender. This and other remains from Maiden Castle can be seen in Dorset County Museum in Dorchester. The Romans later built their own religious sanctuary on the site of the hillfort.

Described by Eric Benfield in his *The Town of Maiden Castle* (1947) as 'one of the greatest defence systems in the British Isles', Maiden Castle still impresses. Its sinuous earthworks flow for 1.5 miles (2.5km) around the contours of the green hill, which commands wonderful views across the surrounding countryside and towards Dorchester.

The coastal section of the AONB runs from Charmouth eastwards, taking in the great 15.5-mile (25km) pebble and shingle spit of Chesil Beach between Abbotsbury and the great limestone headland of the Isle of Portland. The stones of Chesil Beach, which enclose the brackish lagoon and nature reserve known as the Fleet, are graded by the prevailing waves – a process known as longshore drift – so that the stones are smallest at the western end

1

2

3

1 Aerial view of the defences of the Maiden Castle Iron Age hillfort **2** Thomas Hardy's cottage at Higher Bockhampton **3** Swans swimming downstream at Abbotsbury **4** The graded pebbles of Chesil Beach

There are some heights in Wessex,
shaped as if by a kindly hand,
For thinking, dreaming, dying on,
and at crises when I stand,
Say, on Ingpen Beacon eastward,
or on Wylls-Neck westwardly,
I seem where I was before my
birth, and after death may be.

From *Wessex Heights* (1896) by
Thomas Hardy (1840–1928)

1

2

3

THE SIX STUDLAND REPTILES

The Studland Bay NNR is the only place in Britain that is home to all six British species of reptile. It is the rich diversity of the reserve, which includes both dry and wet heathland, that makes it attractive to so many different species.

- Adder: Britain's commonest and only poisonous snake (left)
- Grass snake: the largest snake in Britain and completely harmless
- Sand lizard: the rarest and most beautiful lizard in the country
- Slow worm: not a snake at all but a legless lizard
- Smooth snake: Britain's rarest and shyest snake
- Viviparous, or common, lizard: lays eggs that hatch when deposited

and get progressively bigger as the spit sweeps eastwards towards the limestone headland of Portland Bill. The Fleet is home to the famous Abbotsbury Swannery, said to be the oldest managed swan population in the world, where up to 600 of these regal birds are fed daily, attracting crowds of visitors.

Geology textbook

Portland is the source of the fine white limestone known as Portland Stone, one of the most famous building stones in the world. Many of London's grandest buildings, including St Paul's Cathedral, Buckingham Palace, the Bank of England, the British Museum and the Cenotaph in Whitehall, were built using limestone from Portland.

Both Portland and the seaside town of Weymouth are excluded from the AONB, but the spectacular section of the Dorset coast between Osmington Mills and Studland Bay, overlooking Poole Harbour, comes within the protected area. The great chalk cliffs of White Nothe and Swyre Head are mere preludes to the fantastic natural architecture of the wave-worn flying buttress of Durdle Door, the amazing crumples of Stair Hole, and scallop-shaped Lulworth Cove – a textbook in coastal geology and erosion.

Beyond Lulworth Cove, the AONB opens out past the army training ranges of Lulworth and the Purbeck Marine Wildlife Reserve of Worbarrow Bay and Kimmeridge Bay, to take in the great chalk headland of Purbeck and the sandstone heaths and mudflats of Poole Harbour. The Heritage Coast includes the bold headlands of St Aldhelm's Head, Durlston Head and Handfast Point.

The National Nature Reserve (NNR) of Studland Bay, which is home to all six British species of reptile (see box), is famous for having both dry and wet heathland within its boundaries. Inland is the castle-dominated township of Corfe Castle, defending a significant gap in the limestone ridge of the Purbeck Hills, which reaches the sea at Ballard Point.

Today, Corfe Castle, in the care of the National Trust, is one of Britain's most majestic and evocative ruins, and its fallen walls and secret places make it exciting to explore, especially with children. Its position, controlling a gateway through the Purbeck Hills, made it an important strategic site for William the Conqueror, who built the first castle here soon after his arrival in Britain in 1066. Corfe later became one of King John's favourite castles, and between 1199 and 1216 he added many of the formidable defences and also turned the castle into a comfortable royal residence.

From the 14th to the 16th century, Corfe Castle became less important as a royal stronghold, and it often fell into disrepair. In 1572, Elizabeth I sold it to her Lord Chancellor, Sir Christopher Hatton, who converted it into a prestigious home. The castle was eventually demolished in 1646 by Parliamentarian forces, marking the end of its rich history as both fortress and royal residence.

1 Sunset over spectacular Durdle Door **2** Fossilized rings of algae gathered around tree trunks at Lulworth's Fossil Forest **3** Male adder with distinctive zigzag markings

MENDIP HILLS

The Mendip Hills, honeycombed by caves and mined for centuries for lead, rise as a great 980ft (300m) high limestone barrier above the Somerset Levels and the adjacent Bristol Channel.

From the Bristol Channel, the imposing ridge of the Mendips sweeps eastwards towards the Chew Valley and the cathedral city of Wells. The hills are the southernmost outcrop of Carboniferous limestone in the country, and famous for limestone-loving flora and show caves, such as those at Cheddar Gorge and Wookey Hole.

The Mendips rise to a high, bare plateau around the pretty villages of Priddy and Charterhouse-on-Mendip. Crisscrossed by dry-stone walls and topped by peaty moorland on their summits, the hills can give the impression of belonging much further north.

Designated in 1972, the Mendip Hills AONB covers 76 square miles (198sq km) on the border of the counties of Avon and Somerset. It contains two National Nature Reserves (NNRs) – the beautiful limestone woodlands of the Ebbor Gorge and the famous ash woods of Rodney Stoke – as well as many more Sites of Special Scientific Interest (SSSIs).

The sheer rock faces of the Cheddar Gorge preclude grazing, which makes them among the habitats least affected by humankind in the whole country. For the same reason, they are home to much rare flora, such as the beautiful Cheddar pink, known locally as firewitch – the precipitous Cheddar cliffs remain the only place in Britain where it grows in the wild.

Scrub clearance

Cheddar Gorge is part of the Cheddar Complex SSSI, owned on the southern side by the Longleat Estate, and on the north by the National Trust. Regular scrub clearance keeps bushes and trees from taking over, and Longleat has fenced off a large section of its land and introduced goats as part of a programme to encourage biodiversity. There is also a flock of feral Soay sheep in the gorge.

Notable animals living in Cheddar Gorge include dormice, yellow-necked mice, slow worms and adders, as well as peregrine falcons, buzzards, kestrels, ravens and the rare grasshopper warbler. Insects include the rare large blue butterfly and the small pearl-bordered fritillary.

The gorge is also a nationally important site for whitebeam trees. In 2009, a survey carried out by botanists from the Welsh National Herbarium identified three new species previously unknown to science. These were the Cheddar whitebeam, the Twin Cliffs whitebeam and the Gough's Rock whitebeam, each named after their specific location in the gorge.

Left Looking west from above the Cheddar Gorge, with Cheddar Reservoir and Brent Knoll behind

Although now usually dry, the great limestone gorges of the Mendips, such as Cheddar, Wookey and Ebbor on the southern flanks, and Burrington Combe to the north, were cut by the tremendous erosive force of the meltwater from retreating Ice Age glaciers. Other unique features include the pockmarks of sinkholes and depressions where water has sunk below the surface, water-catching dew ponds and the spectacular show caves at Cheddar and Wookey Hole.

Cheddar Man, Britain's oldest complete human skeleton, estimated to be 9,000 years old, was excavated in Cheddar Gorge in 1903. Since then, archaeologists have found even older remains from around 12,000 to 13,000 years ago (during the Upper Palaeolithic era) both here and at nearby Wookey Hole.

Cheddar Gorge and Wookey Hole, which features the celebrated formation known as the Witch of Wookey (see box), are popular tourist attractions, offering well-lit passages for observing the beautiful stalactites and stalagmites. In a 2005 poll, Cheddar Gorge was named as the second greatest natural wonder in Britain, surpassed only by the Dan-yr-Ogof caves in South Wales. The gorge attracts about 500,000 visitors per year.

The whole AONB is rich in archaeological remains, with nearly 300 barrows, plus field systems, settlements and earthworks dating from the Bronze Age. Among the most impressive prehistoric monuments is the spectacularly sited 17-acre Dolebury Camp. This two-tiered Iron Age hillfort overlooks the village of Churchill and the Bristol Channel at the western end of the Mendips.

At the highest point of Dolebury Camp are the remains of a warrener's (rabbit breeder's) house, but most of the long, barrow-like earthworks found on top of the Mendips turn out to be 'pillow mounds', constructed in medieval times to encourage newly introduced rabbits to breed for meat.

Evidence of lead-mining activity in the Mendips dates back as far as the late Bronze Age, and, as in many other limestone areas of Britain, in Roman times the Mendips became an important centre for lead mining in order to provide plumbing for the Empire. Signs of the industry on the open hills can be seen in the patches of disturbed ground and old mines and adits (shafts), referred to locally as 'gruffy' ground.

Lead legacy

An additional attraction of the lead mines for the Romans was the potential for extracting silver, and the Latin inscription 'EX ARG VEB', found stamped onto Roman pigs of lead from the Mendips, indicates that de-silvering took place here. The silver coinage used by the local Dobunni and Durotriges tribes from that time also points to silver mining taking place.

Perhaps the best remaining example of the Roman lead and silver mines is found at Charterhouse-on-Mendip, where the headquarters of the Mendip Hills AONB is based. These mines were first operated by the Romans in about AD 49. They built a small fort here during the first century AD, and there was also an amphitheatre to entertain the legionaries. The complete 'fossilized' Roman mining landscape at Charterhouse is designated as a Scheduled Ancient Monument.

By the end of the Middle Ages, a system of law had come into existence that covered the four Mendip 'mineries'. Control was in the hands of the monastic foundations, indicating a possible continuity of tenure of the large-scale holdings, focused on the mines, from the Roman period. Mining continued in the Mendips until the Victorian period. Other remains can also be seen in the Blackmoor Nature Reserve, owned by Somerset County Council.

The mainstay of agriculture on the tops of the Mendips today is sheep farming, and Priddy Sheep Fair, which moved to Priddy from Wells during the Black Death in 1348, is held annually on the third Wednesday of August. This is still the occasion for shepherds to buy and sell sheep and show off their breeding flocks. Lower down the slopes, dairy and mixed farming becomes more important, with horticultural holdings on the more fertile southern fringe.

1 Symbolic reconstruction of pens for Priddy Sheep Fair made from 130 ash hurdles **2** The green-smocked auctioneer handles the goods at the Priddy Sheep Fair **3** Inside the caves at Wookey Hole, where one stalagmite is said to be a petrified witch

1

2

THE WITCH OF WOOKEY

The Witch of Wookey is a lifelike, hook-nosed stalagmite in the first chamber of the Wookey Hole caves, and is the central character in a local legend.

The story is that a man from Glastonbury was betrothed to a girl from Wookey, but an oft-jilted and jealous witch living in Wookey Hole caves cursed the romance, so it failed. The man, by now a monk, sought revenge on the witch by stalking her into the cave, where she hid in a dark corner near one of the underground rivers.

The monk blessed the water and splashed some of it into the darkest part of the cave where the witch was hiding. The holy water petrified the witch where she stood, and there she remains to this day.

QUANTOCK HILLS

The views across the West Country from the rolling, wooded slopes of the Quantock Hills, overlooking Bridgwater Bay and the Bristol Channel, are said to extend over nine counties. The Quantock Hills have the distinction of being the first AONB to be designated in England, in 1956, and cover 38 square miles (99sq km) in the districts of Taunton Deane and Sedgemoor in West Somerset.

The 12-mile (19km) ridge of the Quantocks, whose name is thought to come from the ancient British word for a circle, or rim, of hills, always appears more imposing than it really is as it rises suddenly from the flat plain of the Vale of Taunton to the south. The highest point, Will's Neck, near Crowcombe, is only 1,260ft (384m) above sea level, while the average height of this gently curving ridge is between 804ft (245m) and 902ft (275m).

The underlying geology of this mini-range varies from the hard Carboniferous millstone grit of the summits to undulating shales and distinctive New Red Sandstone, which is much more typical of the rest of the West Country. For so small an area, the landscape of the Quantock Hills shows immense variety.

The steep western scarp is deeply cut by combes, which rise to the summit plateau of heathland, a habitat that is now extremely rare in southern Britain. To the east, long broad valleys are enclosed in a landscape of copses and rich hedgerows, which roll gently away to the flat expanse of the Somerset Levels. The hilltops, many of which are open commons with ancient grazing rights, manage to retain a surprising air of solitude and wildness above the soft, sylvan landscapes that surround them.

Quantock staghounds

The sessile oak woodlands of the Quantocks, such as those around Nether Stowey, Holford and Fyne Court, are nationally important and support a wide variety of native species of plants and animals within their shady confines. Many of these woodlands are now protected as local nature reserves.

The wildlife of the Quantocks is justly famous, and ranges from a renowned herd of native red deer to wild ponies of a similar lineage to those of neighbouring Exmoor. The recent history of red deer on the Quantocks is inextricably linked to their being hunted with hounds. Few deer were present on the Quantock Hills before 1862, when Fenwick Bissett, master of the Devon and Somerset Staghounds, introduced red deer, caught on nearby Exmoor. There were several further releases of small numbers over the next 25

1

2

1 The path through the beeches from Triscombe Stone **2** Sign at Coleridge Cottage, Nether Stowey **3** Wild ponies on a Quantock heath **4** The Quantock Staghounds ready to embark on the hunt

3

4

1

years, and in 1901, the Quantock Staghounds was established for hunting, although it was disbanded a few years later. It was in 1917, when only around 30 red deer were present on the hills, that local landowner Sir Dennis Boles was asked to revive the Staghounds by Lloyd George's wartime government. At the same time, the herd was supplemented with several stags brought in from the deer park at Warnham Park in Sussex, and it gradually built up to today's population of several hundred animals.

Although initially concerned purely with sport, the Quantock Staghounds later became involved in culling in a programme of deer management and to help disperse large unwanted herds from farmland. Alongside rifle culls undertaken by individual stalkers, hunting has formed part of local deer management ever since. However, anti-hunting legislation introduced in 2005 no longer allows hunting as traditionally practised with a pack of hounds. A more limited form of 'exempt hunting' is now employed to help flush deer from cover, although the controversial staghounds continue to find and kill injured deer.

High-hedged lanes

Human settlement on the Quantocks can be traced back well into prehistory, with numerous barrows and sites such as the Iron Age hillfort of Danesborough Camp, above Nether Stowey, still very much in evidence.

There are no towns within this AONB, but there are a number of attractive, mainly red sandstone, villages like Combe Florey, East Quantoxhead (which perpetuates the old spelling of the name of the hills) and Crowcombe, all of which are usually reached by narrow, high-hedged lanes.

The poet William Wordsworth lived with his sister Dorothy at Alfoxton House, near Holford, between July 1797 and June 1798, before moving back to their native Lake District. The couple roamed the Quantocks with their friend and fellow poet Samuel Taylor Coleridge, who lived at nearby Nether Stowey in a house now called Coleridge Cottage. Coleridge stayed here for three years from 1797, during which time he wrote some of his best-known work, including *The Rime of the Ancient Mariner*, part of *Christabel*, *Frost at Midnight* and *Kubla Khan*.

The house was acquired for the nation in 1908, and handed over to the National Trust the following year. In 1998, following a £25,000 appeal by the Friends of Coleridge and the Trust, two further rooms on the first floor were officially opened to the public. Incidentally, the 2000 film *Pandaemonium*, based on the lives of Wordsworth and Coleridge, was set in the Quantock Hills.

The rural economy of the Quantocks is based on mixed farming, dominated by dairy farming, sheep and beef cattle. A large part of the Quantocks is still open common land, with traditional grazing rights for local farmers. Forestry and small-scale quarrying are very much secondary activities when compared with agriculture.

Today, however, the Quantocks is also a popular recreational area, much favoured by walkers and horse-riders, who enjoy splendid views once they reach the top. More controversial users include the previously mentioned Quantock Staghounds and, increasingly, trail and mountain bikers.

OTHER AONBs IN THE WEST COUNTRY

The **Cranborne Chase and West Wiltshire Downs** AONB, designated in 1983, covers 380 square miles (983sq km) of sweeping chalk downland, split by deep combes and wooded valleys.

Designated in 1976, the **Scilly Isles**, a granite archipelago consisting of about 100 islands with stunning coastal scenery, cover only 6 square miles (16sq km) and form one of the smallest AONBs.

The beautiful ria (drowned coastline) valleys of the 75 square mile (195sq km) **Tamar Valley** AONB, designated in 1995, discharge into Plymouth Sound.

1 Colourful blooms of heather and gorse mingle on the Quantock Hills, looking towards the Bristol Channel **2** Family groups enjoying the many pathways over the open Quantock heathland **3** Shaped like pieces from a jigsaw puzzle, the Isles of Scilly off the coast of Normandy form one of our smallest AONBs

2

3

THE BEGINNING OF THE END FOR SAXON BRITAIN

It was from Bosham (right) that Harold, Earl of Wessex, set out in 1064 on his ill-fated voyage to Normandy where, after a shipwreck, he unwisely swore an oath of loyalty to Duke William. That ill-judged move was to result in the Norman invasion of 1066 after Harold had been crowned King of England, and to his eventual death at the Battle of Hastings just down the coast.

The original Saxon church at Bosham is featured in one of the earliest panels of the Bayeux tapestry, where Harold is shown at prayer before his fateful voyage. You can still visit the part-Saxon and part-Early English church of Holy Trinity, its original tower now surmounted by a shingled broach spire. The adjacent grassy field known as Quay Meadow, now owned by the National Trust, is allegedly the site from where Harold set sail.

2

1

CHICHESTER HARBOUR

Chichester Harbour is one of the few remaining undeveloped parts of the South Coast of England, an internationally recognized wetland site, and one of Britain's most popular stretches of water for boating. The narrow entrance to the harbour opens out into a landlocked lagoon of low-lying peninsulas, penetrated by a maze of tidal creeks (locally known as 'rithes'), fringed by salt marsh and mud flats.

The small waterside villages, such as West Thorney, Prinsted, West Itchenor and Bosham (pronounced 'Bozzam'), were once busy with commercial craft, but since the harbour silted up in the 19th century, they now provide only a base for yacht and sailing clubs, training centres, and moorings for over 10,000 pleasure boats.

Despite this intense recreational activity, the 28 square mile (73sq km) Chichester Harbour AONB remains an unexpected haven of wildness. Designated in 1963, it encompasses the western shore of Hayling Island and Thorney Island, and consists of farmland leading down to meandering salt marshes and creeks, which are fringed by a woodland margin of oak and hawthorn.

The marshes and flats are the home of many species of wading bird, such as up to 20,000 overwintering dunlin, as well as large flocks of redshank, curlew, bar-tailed and black-tailed godwit, grey plover and sanderling. More than 9,000 brent geese also overwinter on the intertidal mud flats and adjacent farmland. Breeding birds include both the common and sandwich tern, black-headed gull, ringed plover, redshank and shelduck, while the reed beds provide nesting sites for herons and reed buntings. The richness of the wildlife and diverse ecology of the huge tidal mudflats and saltings resulted in the designation of the harbour as an internationally recognized Ramsar wetland site.

The villages that cluster around the harbour, such as Bosham and West Itchenor, add important elements to the landscape. Their church spires, ancient tidal mills and gaily colour-washed and pantiled houses provide welcome focal points. The chief planks of the local economy are the many boatyards, marinas and a little commercial fishing, while the houses in the creekside villages are in huge demand for commuters to nearby Portsmouth and Southampton, or for holiday or retirement accommodation.

The history of Chichester Harbour dates to Saxon times, when Bosham was an important port (see box). A summer ferry still runs from Bosham Hoe across the Chichester channel to West Itchenor.

3

1 Boats moored in Chichester Harbour at low tide **2** Featured in the Bayeux Tapestry, the historic village of Bosham is situated on an inlet of Chichester Harbour **3** Adult black-tailed godwit in spring plumage

CHILTERN HILLS

The chalk escarpment of the Chiltern Hills is one of London's most popular playgrounds, famous for its hanging beech woods and brick-and-flint villages, which are now in high demand as homes for city commuters. The escarpment is also followed by the ancient Ridgeway, now a National Trail, which threads its way southwest from Ivinghoe Beacon towards Wallington and the Thames Valley, and eventually all the way to Wiltshire (see box).

Where prehistoric man once used this chalky highway to escape the terrors of the deeply wooded Vale of Aylesbury and the London Basin, walkers today now enjoy some of the finest views in the southeast of England. The Chilterns make ideal walking country, with an unparalleled network of public rights of way leading across the hills and through the woods. The 322 square mile (833sq km) Chiltern Hills AONB was designated in 1964.

These airy uplands were obviously very important to ancient man, and the landscape retains many other traces of their presence, such as the great defensive dyke of Grim's Ditch, running north from Lacey Green to Great Hampden, and the Roman Icknield Way, which runs parallel to the Ridgeway.

Grim's Ditch, which is usually dated to the Iron Age, runs for a total length of 25 miles (40km) through the Chilterns. It is not continuous but has a number of large gaps, presumably originally filled in by the forest or by fences. It is thought to have been a

1 A sweeping panoramic view of the Chiltern Hills from Coombe Hill **2** Attractive brick-and-flint cottages in Turville village, with Cobstone Windmill beyond

1

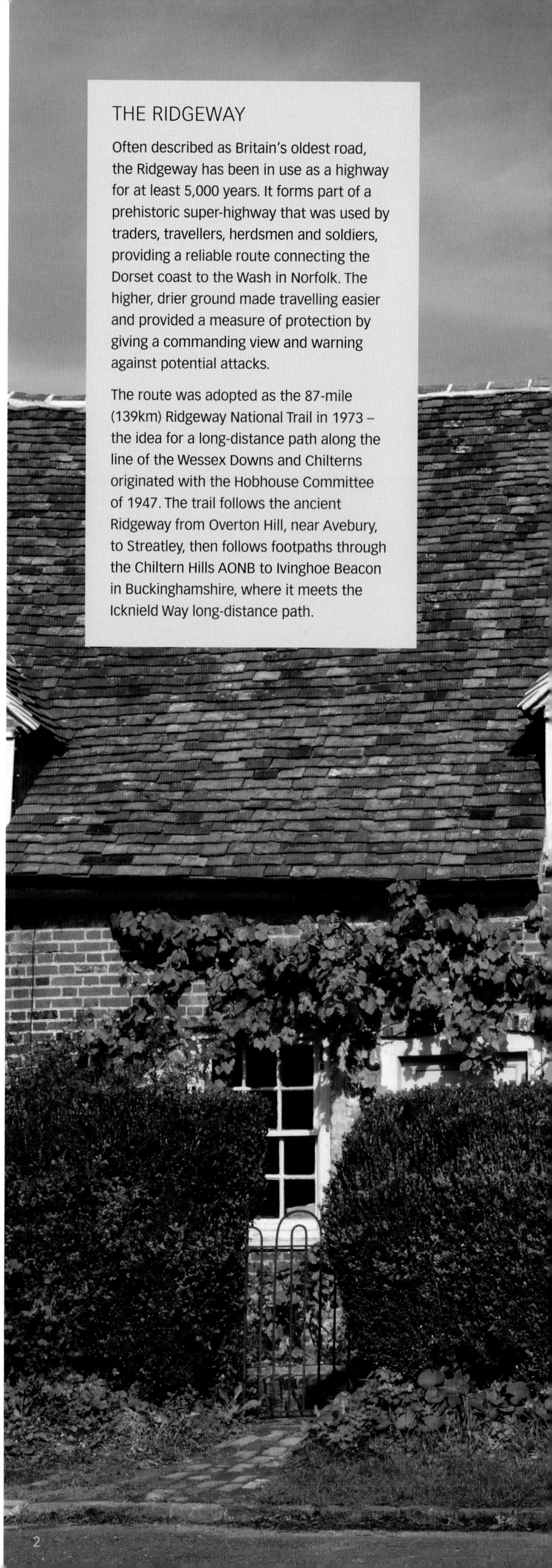

THE RIDGEWAY

Often described as Britain's oldest road, the Ridgeway has been in use as a highway for at least 5,000 years. It forms part of a prehistoric super-highway that was used by traders, travellers, herdsmen and soldiers, providing a reliable route connecting the Dorset coast to the Wash in Norfolk. The higher, drier ground made travelling easier and provided a measure of protection by giving a commanding view and warning against potential attacks.

The route was adopted as the 87-mile (139km) Ridgeway National Trail in 1973 – the idea for a long-distance path along the line of the Wessex Downs and Chilterns originated with the Hobhouse Committee of 1947. The trail follows the ancient Ridgeway from Overton Hill, near Avebury, to Streatley, then follows footpaths through the Chiltern Hills AONB to Ivinghoe Beacon in Buckinghamshire, where it meets the Icknield Way long-distance path.

2

1

2

3

4

boundary constructed by the local Celtic tribe, known as the Catuvellauni. The best-preserved stretches of Grim's Ditch can be seen at Great Hampden, near the church, and there is another fine length on Pitstone Hill.

Rich tapestry of habitats

In view of its proximity to London and the fact that 8.5 million people are estimated to live within 25 miles (40km) – or easy day-trip distance – of the Chilterns, this highly pressured area succeeds through careful management to remain astonishingly rural and retain its sense of timeless beauty. This is especially true in the spring, when the floors of the beautiful hanging beech woods of the Chilterns become blanketed with a misty blue carpet of bluebells, or in autumn, when the 'carpet' changes colour to a crisp golden pile created by discarded beech leaves.

Britain is the only country in Europe where bluebell woods, like those found in the Chilterns, are commonplace. And the argument continues as to whether we should regard the beech as a native tree – it has been around for at least 5,000 years, and humankind has made good use of it during that time. But beech is certainly a southerner because it does not generally reproduce naturally north of the Midlands and South Wales.

On the open chalk downland, such as around Ivinghoe Beacon, the grasslands provide important habitats for insects, particularly butterflies, and in the damp valley bottoms, wetlands provide yet another home for wildlife. This rich tapestry of habitats has resulted in many parts of the Chiltern Hills AONB being designated nature reserves. These include the chalk downland and beech woodlands of Grangelands and Pulpit Hill, and the National Trust's Coombe Hill Nature Trail, where the views extend across to the Cotswolds and the Berkshire Downs.

The Chilterns are dissected by the M40 motorway at the deep cutting of Stokenchurch Gap, between junctions 5 and 6. Known locally as 'the Canyon', this controversial cutting slices through the chalk bedrock in a spectacular fashion. However, observant motorists near Stokenchurch Gap are often able to witness the results of one of the greatest success stories in the conservation of Chiltern and, indeed, British wildlife.

Soaring above the incessant roar of the motorway are the elegant, fork-tailed shapes of russet-brown red kites, an endangered species brought back from the edge of extinction by enlightened conservation policies. Common even in cities such as London in Tudor times, red kites were driven to extinction in England, mainly as a result of human persecution, by the end of the 19th century.

A small population survived in Wales, but there was little chance of these birds repopulating their original areas unaided.

1 Woodland on the Ashridge Estate suffused with sunshine on an autumn day **2** Britain is the only country in Europe where bluebell woods, like these in Ashridge Forest, are commonplace **3** Chalkhill blue butterflies resting on the distinctive Chiltern gentian flowers **4** A red kite soars over Watlington Hill

Then, between 1989 and 1994, kites from Spain were released into the Chilterns by the RSPB and English Nature. The kites started breeding in the Chilterns in 1992 and there are now thought to be over 300 breeding pairs in the area. Indeed, since 1999, chicks have been taken from the Chilterns to reintroduce these handsome raptors to other parts of the country.

Film locations

The latest threat to the Chilterns AONB is the proposed new HS2 high-speed rail link between London and Birmingham, which has been opposed by the Chilterns Conservation Board and many local people. The proposed route would pass through the Misbourne Valley, past Chalfont St Giles, Amersham and Wendover, slicing through one of the most scenic valleys in the Chilterns AONB.

The AONB boundary avoids the towns of Luton, Reading, High Wycombe and Hemel Hempstead but, nevertheless, about 100,000 people live and work in the area. Traditional industries have included furniture making, or 'bodging', based in High Wycombe and using the abundant, locally cut beech wood (see box).

The villages within the AONB are mainly built of local brick and flint. Thanks to careful planning, these villages have managed to keep their unique Chiltern character, and they seem to rise almost organically from the surrounding countryside. Typical examples of these villages are Turville, Little Missenden, Pyrton and The Lee.

Film and television viewers, particularly fans of the popular BBC comedy series *The Vicar of Dibley*, may recognize the pretty village of Turville, which lies in the heart of the Chilterns, about 5 miles (8km) west of High Wycombe. It features in most of the outdoor scenes in the *Dibley* series, which starred Dawn French as the first female vicar in a typically conservative English village. In the programme, the church was named St Barnabas but, in fact, it is dedicated to St Mary the Virgin. Like many Chiltern villages, Turville is Anglo-Saxon in origin. Its name means 'dry field', and it was first recorded in the *Anglo-Saxon Chronicle* in 796 as Thyrefeld.

Overlooking the village is Cobstone Windmill, also known as Turville and Ibstone Windmill, which is actually in the neighbouring parish of Ibstone. A smock mill, built in 1816, it replaced the original mill that had stood there since the 16th century. It was a working mill grinding cereal until 1873, and featured in the popular 1968 musical film, *Chitty Chitty Bang Bang*.

The Chilterns have a fine sense of history. The 17th-century mansion of Hampden House in Great Hampden was the home of the early democrat John Hampden, whose refusal to pay the ship money tax to Charles I was one of the catalysts of the Civil War. Hampden fought with the Parliamentarians and died at the Battle of Chalgrove Field in 1643. He is buried in the churchyard of St Mary Magdalene, within the parkland of Hampden House.

1 The National Trust's Ashridge Estate runs northwest up to Ivinghoe Beacon **2** Cobstone Windmill is a landmark above Turville **3** Old man's beard, also known as traveller's joy or wild clematis **4** Bronze statue of John Hampden, whose defiance of King Charles I was one of the causes of the Civil War, in Aylesbury Market Square

1

2

BODGING

Today, the word 'bodging' or 'to bodge' is generally used in connection with poor or clumsy workmanship. But for many centuries in the Chiltern beech woods, a 'bodger' was a highly skilled craftsman who specialized in making chair legs and braces.

The craft of bodging goes back at least 500 years. The bodger would select a leggy (quickly grown) beech tree, and with the aid of his tools, usually a saw, an axe, chisels, a drawknife and a lathe (traditionally, a pole lathe, made of nothing more than springy wood and string), he would create the chair legs.

Bodgers usually worked in isolation in temporary workshops in the woodlands where the trees were felled. The finished chair legs would be left in the woods to season for a few weeks, then taken to a furniture-making centre, like nearby High Wycombe, for making up into chairs.

3

4

KENT DOWNS

The White Cliffs of Dover are an English icon – the epitome of our island heritage and sense of nationhood. They also mark the point where the Kent Downs AONB, that great arc of chalk downland stretching from the Surrey Hills and sometimes known as 'the Garden of England', finally reaches the sea.

Ever since the time of the Romans, the North Downs have provided a high-level highway to the capital, and also a convenient route for successive invaders of England, most notably William the Conqueror in 1066. In the reverse direction, they also provided a relatively safe passage for pilgrims from London, such as those in Chaucer's *The Canterbury Tales,* down to the holy shrine of St Thomas Becket at Canterbury (see box, page 53).

The Kent Downs AONB was officially designated in 1967 and covers 339 square miles (878sq km) of the North Downs. This is a well-ordered and settled landscape, where chalk and greensand escarpments look down into the wooded Weald to the south. The main industry is farming on the high-grade and fertile soils, and horticulture is also still important in the famous hop fields and orchards of North and East Kent.

Generations of chirpy Eastenders made the annual migration from London to the hop fields of Kent in September before and just after World War II to pick the hops, which are an essential ingredient of beer.

Kent's most famous crop was introduced to the county during the 16th century, and by 1724 there were 6,000 acres of hop gardens in East Kent. The hops have to be encouraged to find their way up the slender wooden frames, known as strings, so in springtime the new shoots have to be trained, or 'twiddled', to encourage them to climb.

Kent's agricultural economy always needed a large temporary workforce to gather in the hops and, by the end of the last century, up to 250,000 extra pickers were employed, about a third of whom came from the East End of London. Others came from travelling bands of local Romanies. For these travellers, hop-picking was often followed by fruit- and, finally, potato-picking. Today, most of this work is undertaken by specialist picking machines or by foreign students, who are often accommodated in bunkhouses on the farms, just as the Cockneys once were.

Kentish manors

Rising to over 590ft (180m), the chalk and greensand ridges of the Kent Downs are generally well wooded with native broadleaved

1 Walkers on the Saxon Shore Way peer over the white cliffs of Dover **2** Oast houses in the Kent countryside **3** Generations of Londoners spent their holidays picking Kentish hops in the 1950s **4** A shady path along the Saxon Shore Way

2

3

4

1

2

3

trees and some permanent unimproved grasslands, which are extremely valuable as wildlife habitats. The greensand ridge in the vicinity of the commuter towns of Sevenoaks and Maidstone (both of which are excluded from the AONB) is particularly rich in native tree cover.

The abundance of oaks in the area in medieval times gave rise to the many half-timbered buildings still found in the AONB. Typical is the Kentish yeoman farmer's house, with its central hall, jutting eaves and projecting upper storeys, which usually marked the home of a prosperous landowner.

Ightham Mote, on a by-road near Sevenoaks, is a perfect example of a 14th- or 15th-century Kentish moated manor house, beautifully set among lush trees and meadows. Dating from 1320, Ightham Mote was described by the architectural critic Nikolaus Pevsner as 'the most complete small medieval manor house in the country', and it remains a rare example of how such houses would have looked in the Middle Ages.

The importance of Ightham Mote lies in the fact that successive owners made relatively few changes to the main structure, after the completion of the quadrangle with a new chapel in the 16th century. It was bequeathed to the National Trust in 1985 by the American businessman Charles Henry Robinson, who had bought it in 1953. The house is now a Grade I listed building, and parts of it are also a Scheduled Ancient Monument.

Many historic parklands, including Knole Park and Sir Winston Churchill's red-brick former home at Chartwell, are also included within the AONB. The area is also crossed by the 153-mile (246km) North Downs Way National Trail, which runs from Rochester through to Dover, making a much more pleasant parallel to the roaring traffic on the M20 motorway.

Attractive settlements such as Charing, site of Archbishop Cranmer's Tudor palace, and Chilham, with its magnificent half-timbered buildings and 17th-century castle built on a Norman site, can be found on the Pilgrim's Way, the traditional route for Canterbury-bound pilgrims in the Middle Ages.

The Kent Downs AONB is bordered by large and expanding urban areas, including Ashford, Sevenoaks and the Medway towns of Rochester, Chatham and Gillingham. The coming of the M20 and high-speed rail links to the Channel Tunnel at Dover have brought even more pressure on this fragile, protected landscape.

Yet in the nature reserves, such as the traditionally coppiced woodlands of Denge Wood and Earley Wood, and the ancient fine chalk woodland of Yockletts Bank high on the North Downs near Ashford, it is still possible to experience the atmosphere of wilderness that must have been felt by the earliest travellers along this ancient ridgeway.

1 Purple toadflax growing along the Saxon Shore Way **2** Ightham Mote **3** A fallow deer buck in Knole Park **4** Illustration of pilgrims embarking on their journey in Chaucer's classic 14th-century story *The Canterbury Tales* **5** The soaring pinnacles of Canterbury Cathedral

4

THE CANTERBURY TALES

The Canterbury Tales is a collection of stories written in Middle English by Geoffrey Chaucer at the end of the 14th century. It was the first large-circulation book to be printed in English by William Caxton, the father of English printing, in around 1476.

The tales are told mostly in verse, although two are in prose, and form a storytelling contest by a group of pilgrims, including larger-than-life characters such as the Wife of Bath, the Knight and the Monk. They travel together on the journey from Southwark in London along the Kent Downs to the shrine of St Thomas Becket at Canterbury Cathedral. They would probably have travelled along Watling Street, an ancient route even in Chaucer's time. The stretch from London to Canterbury and then on to Dover is now followed by the A2.

5

SURREY HILLS

Spanning the length of Surrey from east to west, the Surrey Hills include popular walking destinations such as the Devil's Punch Bowl and Box Hill, and provide a vital 'lung' for the citizens of South London.

The hills are largely formed of the dazzling white chalk of the North Downs, which rise near Guildford as the narrow Hog's Back and stretch away eastwards to the border with Kent, near Limpsfield. To the west and on the Hampshire border is the sandy, heathery heathland of Frensham Common.

Parallel to the south of the downs is the undulating, richly wooded greensand ridge, which rises to tower-topped Leith Hill, at 965ft (294m) the highest point in southeast England. The summit of Leith Hill is distinguished by Richard Hull's 18th-century Gothic tower, which affords a panoramic view north towards London and south to the English Channel 25 miles (40km) away. On a clear day, the view takes in 13 counties (14, if you include Greater London).

The somewhat eccentric Hull, of nearby Leith Hill Place, built the tower, which he called his Prospect House, between 1765 and 1766. He objected to the fact that his local hill stood a little short of the magical figure of 1,000ft (305m) above sea level. However, by building the 64ft (19.5m) tower, the problem was solved – the top of the tower stands 1,029ft (314m) above the sea.

Front-line AONB

The AONB covers a total of 162 square miles (419sq km) and was designated in 1956. The former Countryside Commission once described the Surrey Hills as a 'front-line AONB', regarding it as the beleaguered last thin green line holding back the sprawling suburbanization creeping out from South London.

Places like Box Hill, the Devil's Punch Bowl (see box, page 57) and Leith Hill are popular weekend day-out destinations for Londoners and people from the towns in the southeast. The villages within the AONB are highly desirable for commuters to the metropolis, making property prices extremely high.

The AONB links a chain of varied landscapes, from the narrow 492ft (150m) high ridge of the Hog's Back, which is followed by the A31 road between Farnham and Guildford, to the swelling hills and beech-clad combes of the North Downs, with their steep scarp crest overlooking the Weald to the south. Running to the south of the downs is the gently undulating greensand ridge, and in the extreme west, the heathlands of Frensham Common.

It is the fine deciduous woodlands and chalk grasslands that give the Surrey Hills their unique quality, but equally important are the heathlands and native Scots pines of the heaths, as seen around the Devil's Punch Bowl at Hindhead on the A3 and on the

Right The extensive view from Friday Street, Leith Hill

1

2

3

4

THE DEVIL'S PUNCH BOWL

There are several legends about how the great natural amphitheatre known as the Devil's Punch Bowl, on the A3 near Hindhead, got its name. The most usual is that the Devil became so annoyed by the number of churches being built in Sussex that he decided to dig a channel from the English Channel clean through the South Downs to flood them out.

But when he got as far as the area still known as Devil's Dyke near Poynings, he was disturbed by a cock crowing. Assuming that dawn was about to break, he leapt across the border into Surrey, creating the great hole known as the Devil's Punch Bowl when he landed.

Another version states that the Devil was hurling lumps of earth at the pagan god Thor to annoy him, and the hollow from which he scooped the earth became the Punch Bowl. Coincidentally, the name of the local village of Thursley means 'the clearing dedicated to Thor'. Another story claims that two giants clashed in the area, and one, grabbing earth to throw at the other, created the landmark before overshooting his target and inadvertently creating the Isle of Wight in the Solent.

sandy soils of Frensham Common. All these are extremely rare habitats in the southeast of England and thus vitally important for both their flora and fauna, which makes the undergrounding of the A3 currently under construction at Hindhead particularly welcome.

Frensham Common, near Farnham, is one of the last truly wild places in the southeast, and features the Great Pond and Little Pond, two of the largest lakes in the region, which are used for sailing, fishing and birdwatching. Box Hill has been a popular picnic place since the reign of Charles II, when the diarist John Evelyn praised its yews and the box trees after which it is named. Many of those box trees, famous for the hardness of their wood, were cut down in the 18th century and used for wood-engraving blocks by artists such as Thomas Bewick of Northumberland.

The built environment of the Surrey Hills is equally precious, and there are several showpiece villages such as Abinger, which retains its stocks and whipping post and a part-Norman church, and Shere, an attractive village on the River Tillingbourne under the escarpment of the North Downs.

Close to Abinger is its sister village of Abinger Hammer – the suffix recalls the forge hammers of the 17th-century iron industry that flourished in this part of the hills. The introduction of new furnace technology in the early 17th century led to the expansion of the iron industry in the Weald, where rich deposits of iron ore had been exploited since prehistoric times. But by the end of the century, all the local mines had been worked out.

Abinger Hammer is also famous for its eccentric clock tower, which overhangs the main street. The tower was erected in memory of Lord Farrer, who lived at Abinger Hall, and also commemorates the association of Abinger Hammer with the iron industry through the figure of an ironworker striking the bell.

The towns of Guildford, Epsom, with its famous racecourse, Sutton and Reigate are excluded from the AONB, but the Greensand Way and North Downs Way long-distance footpaths run through it, and there is an extensive network of other rights of way.

OTHER AONBs IN THE SOUTH OF ENGLAND

The high sandstone ridges, thickly wooded valleys and patchwork-quilt fields of the 564 square mile (1,460sq km) **High Weald** AONB were designated in 1983. The **Isle of Wight** is a large island in the Solent, with chalk downland in the south and centre and a spectacular coastline, popular with holidaymakers. A total of 73 square miles (189sq km) of the island were designated an AONB in 1963. The bare, chalky uplands of the **North Wessex Downs** were designated an AONB in 1972 and are centred on the town of Marlborough and the River Kennet. The 668 square miles (1,730sq km) of the AONB are rich in prehistoric remains.

1 The poisonous red-capped fly agaric toadstool growing on Gibbet Hill, near Hindhead **2** Red brick wall with embedded flints at Shere **3** The Abinger Hammer village sign depicts its long-standing connections with the iron industry
4 Frensham Little Pond in autumn

2

3

1

DEDHAM VALE

Inescapably associated with the landscape artist John Constable, the Dedham Vale AONB (population just over 8,000) is centred on the valley of the River Stour and the villages of Dedham, Stratford St Mary and Nayland on the Essex–Suffolk border. The AONB, which covers 35 square miles (90sq km) of the Stour Valley to the north of Colchester, was designated in 1970.

John Constable was born in East Bergholt in 1776. He is so closely associated with the area that it is now widely known as Constable Country. The AONB designation has probably protected it from the worst theme park development, although the pressure of tourism remains one of the greatest threats to it.

Unspoiled areas like the valley of the River Stour are rare in East Anglia. The landscape created by the slow-moving, meandering river, with tall-hedged water meadows watched over by drooping willows and stately poplars, used to be common in lowland Britain, but the increasing mechanization of agriculture has resulted in the disappearance of much of it. However, visitors to the area can still see the countryside that inspired Constable, one of the fathers of Impressionism, and modern-day artists can enrol in painting courses at Flatford Mill and Willy Lott's Cottage, the subjects of some of Constable's most famous paintings.

The area of the AONB runs inland from the Stour estuary at Manningtree and takes in both banks of the river, which at this point marks the county boundary between Essex and Suffolk. It includes the villages of Dedham, whose 16th-century church tower provides the focal point of so many of Constable's paintings; Stratford St Mary, where the church stands isolated across the busy dual carriageway of the A12; Polstead; Nayland; and Stoke-by-Nayland. All these villages contain fine examples of half-timbered and thatched cottages and magnificent churches, reflecting their heyday during the 14th century, when this part of East Anglia was one of the richest and most heavily populated parts of England and the headquarters of the wool industry.

The AONB designation was made chiefly to protect the landscape of this highly pressurized area. East Anglia's traditional grasslands, where the 'golden fleeces' of medieval sheep once grazed, are mostly gone now, replaced by the grim monoculture of prairie grain farming. That puts the deep hedgerows and unimproved wildflower water meadows of Dedham Vale among some of the country's rarest and most precious habitats. Field studies are conducted at places such as Flatford Mill to teach people the importance of retaining these ancient landscapes.

4

1 Flatford Mill and pond **2** *Dedham Vale*, *c.*1802 (oil on canvas), by John Constable (1776–1837) **3** Colourful 16th-century houses at Nayland **4** Rowing boats moored along the River Stour at Dedham

LINCOLNSHIRE WOLDS

The Lincolnshire Wolds give the lie to anyone who thought that this area of Britain was predominantly flat. These attractive, rolling chalk hills, stretching for 40 miles (64km) between the Wash and the Humber estuary, emphatically contradict the common belief that the county of Lincolnshire consists solely of low-lying fens and swampy marshland.

Reaching a height of over 550ft (168m) near Normanby-le-Wold, the Lincolnshire Wolds AONB was designated in 1973, and covers 215 square miles (558sq km) of gentle chalk hills, deep valleys and hanging beech woods. Geologically speaking, the wolds were formed from a dissected chalk plateau, a northern extension of the Jurassic chalk ridges of the Chilterns and Berkshire Downs, and fall gently towards the east from a western scarp slope that overlooks the Midland plain.

Lightly populated, the Lincolnshire Wolds have long been famous for the 'golden fleeces' of their many sheep, traditionally the shaggy, curly-fleeced Lincoln Longwool breed. One of Britain's oldest and rarest sheep breeds, it is also one of the biggest, and produces a lustrous fleece that is in great demand for sheepskin rugs. The Lincoln Longwool was used by the noted 18th-century breeder Robert Bakewell to produce the Dishley Leicester breed, and has been exported widely, especially to Argentina, Eastern Europe and Australasia.

Arable farming is also very important on the Lincolnshire Wolds, with the picking of the early-harvested crops of wheat and peas continuing through the night at the peak of the season. In the north of the area, vegetable farming is increasingly important to feed the frozen food factories of Grimsby and Humberside.

Tennyson country

This is prosperous farming country, reflected in the well-kept farmhouses and red pantiled villages, such as Somersby, birthplace of the Victorian Poet Laureate Alfred, Lord Tennyson (see box, page 62), and Old Bolingbroke, perhaps the finest of the Wolds villages. Henry IV, son of John of Gaunt, was born in the now-destroyed castle at Old Bolingbroke in 1367. Somersby, at the southern end of the Wolds, has become the centre of so-called 'Tennyson Country', and you can still see the rectory (in private hands) where the popular poet was born. Tennyson was the son of the rector of Somersby, and the fourth of 12 children. He and two of his

1 The 294ft (90m) high spire of St James parish church at Louth has been described as one of the last Gothic masterpieces of the Middle Ages **2** Towers of oat straw bales add architecture to the Lincolnshire Wolds **3** Lincoln Longwool sheep

1

2

3

TENNYSON'S LEGACY

A surprising number of everyday phrases in the English language were coined by Alfred, Lord Tennyson. They include: 'Nature, red in tooth and claw'; ''Tis better to have loved and lost, than never to have loved at all'; 'Theirs not to reason why, Theirs but to do and die'; and 'The old order changeth, yielding place to new'.

Tennyson is, after William Shakespeare, the second most frequently quoted writer in *The Oxford Dictionary of Quotations*. Among his most popular poems were *The Lady of Shalott, The Charge of the Light Brigade, Tears, Idle Tears* and his blank verse, much of which was based on classical mythology, including *Idylls of the King, Ulysses* and *Tithonus.*

elder brothers were already writing poems in their teens, and a collection of them was published locally when Alfred was only 17. He was educated at Louth Grammar School and entered Trinity College, Cambridge, in 1827. But, in 1831, he was forced to leave Cambridge before taking his degree when his father died, and he returned to the rectory.

In 1833, Tennyson published his second book of poetry, which included his well-known poem *The Lady of Shalott*. The book was heavily criticized, which so discouraged Tennyson that he did not publish another for a decade, although he continued to write. He eventually moved to London, where he was appointed Poet Laureate after William Wordsworth's death in 1850.

Many village names on the Wolds have endings in 'by' or 'thorpe'. This reflects their founding by invading Viking Danes in the 9th century – *by* in Old Norse means a settlement, and *thorpe* is a farmstead belonging to a village. Examples of these villages are Asterby, Goulceby, Scamblesby, Scrivelsby and Winceby, and the famous fishing port of Grimsby on the Humber. The 'thorpes' include Cawthorpe and the seaside resorts of Mablethorpe and Cleethorpes, just outside the AONB on the North Sea coast.

History is everywhere on these pleasantly rolling hills, and there is a wealth of prehistoric barrows and ancient tracks, such as the 147-mile (237km) Viking Way long-distance footpath, which runs from the banks of the Humber at Barton-upon-Humber, across the Wolds to Caistor, then along the valley of the River Bain to Horncastle, and on to Woodhall Spa and, eventually, to Lincoln.

There is also a large number of deserted medieval villages in the AONB, abandoned usually not because of the commonly given reason of the Black Death, but deliberately depopulated by wealthy landowners to make room for more profitable sheep. Examples of these deserted villages are Beesby, North Cadeby, Cawkwell and East and West Wykeham.

Much of the traditional open grassland and hedged fields of the Wolds has now been ploughed up to create the lucrative prairies required by modern arable farming. But where the old pastureland survives in the steep-sided valleys or in deserted chalk pits, important habitats still exist for rare flowers, such as orchids, and their dependent insects, including butterflies.

There still remain some areas of fine old mixed woodlands, carefully managed to retain and conserve their traditional oak,

1

2

3

4

ash and hazel coppices, such as Nettleton Wood, south of Caistor, now owned by the Woodland Trust, which is based in Grantham. Nettleton Wood was purchased by the Trust in 1981 and is a mixture of young birch, oak and grassy heathland.

The 'capital' and communications centre for the Wolds is Louth, just outside the AONB; it is, nevertheless, one of the most perfectly preserved Georgian towns in England. Situated where the ancient trackway known as Barton Street crosses the River Lud, it has a population of nearly 16,000.

The shapely spire of St James's church in Louth dates from the 16th century and is made of Ancaster stone. It is one of the great landmarks of the Wolds. Westgate is one of the town's finest streets, while the Greenwich Meridian crosses Eastgate and is marked with a plaque on the north side of the street, east of the junction with Northgate.

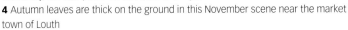

1 Poppies mingle with the wheat crop in the Lincolnshire Wolds **2** The rectory at Somersby, the birthplace of Alfred, Lord Tennyson **3** Burnt orchids on the Wolds **4** Autumn leaves are thick on the ground in this November scene near the market town of Louth

1

2

3

NORFOLK COAST

The North Norfolk Coast is one of East Anglia's wildest and remotest spots – a country of wide skies, ever-changing horizons, and a wealth of wildlife habitats, from marshland to sand dunes and shingle spits.

Some of Europe's finest stretches of coastal marshes are included in the Norfolk Coast AONB, which runs from the Wash to the clay cliffs of Weybourne, taking in most of the northern coast of Norfolk. The AONB – 174 square miles (451sq km) in extent – was designated in 1967 to protect this precious and rare habitat. Since then, 40 miles (64km) of the coastline have been designated as the North Norfolk Heritage Coast, which is also a Ramsar wetland (protected under the international Ramsar Convention on wetlands), a Biosphere Reserve, a Site of Special Scientific Interest (SSSI), and a European Special Protection Area for birds.

The AONB runs in a long coastal strip from the silty, wet wilderness of the Wash, north of King's Lynn, taking in the shining, north-facing coastal marshes and dunes of the Heritage Coast between Hunstanton and Cley-next-the-Sea, to the fast-eroding but surprisingly high boulder clay cliffs east of Weybourne and the border with the Norfolk and Suffolk Broads National Park.

The coastline is backed by gently rolling and highly fertile chalklands and glacial moraines, including the 295ft (90m) high Cromer Ridge, near the seaside town of the same name. The constantly shifting coastline is of unique scientific and ecological interest, and contains some of the most important salt marsh, intertidal flats and lagoons, sand dunes, shingle and grazing marshlands in the whole of Europe.

Round towers and windmills

Nature reserves within the AONB include the world-famous bird reserve of Scolt Head Island, a shingle, dune and salt-marsh island, with access only by prior arrangement with local boatmen from Holme-next-the-Sea or Burnham Overy Staithe; the wide sandy expanses of Holkham Beach; the clenched shingle fist of Blakeney Point, famous for its grey and common seals; Winterton Dunes, which are one of the country's finest unspoilt dune systems and the home of rough-legged buzzards and little terns; and the RSPB's Titchwell Marsh, near Thornham, best known for its avocets and other waders.

The area is characterized by quiet, brick-and-flint villages, such as Wells-next-the-Sea, Holme-next-the-Sea, Cley-next-the-Sea, Brancaster, Blakeney and Burnham Deepdale. The 'next-the-Sea' appellation shouldn't always be taken literally, however, because

1 The two-tone cliffs at Hunstanton **2** Rippling shingle patterns on the beach at Holkham Bay **3** Common seals basking in the sun at Blakeney Point **4** Windswept dunes at Holkham Bay

COKE OF NORFOLK

Thomas William Coke, Earl of Leicester (1754–1842), is widely regarded as one of the main forces behind the British Agricultural Revolution. He is particularly credited with improvements made to animal breeding and cattle, sheep and pig husbandry.

Working on his Holkham estate, Coke pioneered the most advanced methods of animal husbandry from 1776 until his death in 1842. Farmers from all over Britain and overseas would attend his annual three-day gatherings – known as the Holkham Clippings – which were held on the estate at sheep-shearing time. In many ways, these gatherings were the forerunners of modern agricultural shows.

1

2

3

4

the villages of Cley (pronounced 'Clay' or, locally, 'Cly') and Holme are now quite a distance inland, due to land reclamation and the silting-up of their ancient harbours.

Many of these unspoilt villages have imposing, often circular, church towers, such as that at Burnham Deepdale, one of six medieval churches found within 2 miles (3.2km) of each other. The reason for the distinctive round towers, which are so common in Norfolk, was not, as is often stated, that they were a form of defence against invaders, but simply because the absence of any other workable building stone made local flint the best available building material. This knobbly and uneven stone, usually 'knapped' (hammered and split open) to reveal its black interior, was easier to build into circular towers than masonry-faced square ones.

Another distinguishing feature of the built landscape of north Norfolk is the white-sailed windmills, such as the 18th-century red-brick tower mill at Cley-next-the-Sea. These windmills were often used not to grind corn, as is usually assumed, but to drain the salt marshes to create more land for agriculture. The master of land reclamation was Thomas William Coke of Holkham Hall, known as Coke of Norfolk (see box). He was Britain's foremost agriculturalist in the 18th century and reclaimed a great deal of new land around Cley, Blakeney and Wells.

Holkham Hall, described by Simon Jenkins in *England's Thousand Best Houses* (2003) as 'the perfect English house from the Golden Age of the Grand Tour', was built by an earlier Thomas Coke, the 1st Earl of Leicester, in the mid-18th century. Still the ancestral home of the Coke family, the house survives little altered from the original design. The grand, Palladian-style house is said to reflect the first Thomas's appreciation of classical art, which he developed during his six-year-long Grand Tour of Europe. He employed architect Matthew Brettingham to oversee the work of implementing the designs for the new house, which had been drawn up by William Kent and himself. Work started in 1734 and the house was completed 30 years later. Unfortunately, Thomas never saw the realization of his great dream because he died in 1759.

The holiday resorts of Hunstanton, with its multicoloured striped cliffs of alternate bands of white and red chalk and brown sandstone, and Cromer and Sheringham, where the sea is constantly reclaiming land through fierce coastal erosion, are excluded from the AONB. The whole of the North Norfolk coast is a popular holiday area for those from the Midlands and London, and sailing is a common pursuit in the creeks and on the North Sea.

The 93-mile (150km) National Trail of the Norfolk Coast Path, which links to the ancient Peddars Way and terminates at Holme-next-the-Sea, passes through the AONB, providing exhilarating walking along the surprisingly wild and often windswept coastline. The route was officially opened by the Prince of Wales in 1986.

1 Walker on the Norfolk Coast Path at Cley-next-the-Sea **2** Acrobatics from a bearded tit at Titchwell Marsh RSPB Reserve **3** The brick-built tower windmill at Cley-next-the-Sea **4** River Glaven flowing through Cley marshes, Cley-next-the-Sea

1

2

3

4

SUFFOLK COAST & HEATHS

Suffolk is traditionally thought of as flat and uninteresting, but the Suffolk Coast and Heaths emphatically are not. Some of the last wild lowland heaths in England sweep down to reed-fringed creeks, shingle spits and salt marshes, which are the home of many rare birds.

The Suffolk Coast and Heaths AONB was designated in 1969 and covers 156 square miles (403sq km) between Lowestoft in the north and Felixstowe to the south. It includes 35 miles (57km) of the Suffolk Heritage Coast and three National Nature Reserves (NNRs), plus the famous Minsmere RSPB Reserve.

The AONB protects heathland, sand marsh and mud flats, all of which are now seriously threatened habitats in lowland Britain. The coast is deeply indented by the slow-flowing estuaries of the rivers Blyth, Alde, Deben, Orwell and Stour, and is bounded by crumbling low sea cliffs and tidal shingle spits, which constantly fight a battle against the ever-encroaching North Sea.

The Suffolk coast is particularly important for wildlife in Britain, as evidenced by the various protected areas. Minsmere is probably the RSPB's most famous reserve, where that rare and elegant wader, the black-and-white avocet, returned some years ago in one of the Society's greatest success stories. These birds now form one of the biggest breeding colonies in Britain. Also seen on the Scrape – an artificial shallow lagoon – are other rarities, such as the exotic spoonbill and the purple heron, while marsh harriers float effortlessly above the swaying reed beds. Nearly 300 species of bird have been recorded at Minsmere.

The Suffolk Coast NNR (centred around the village of Walberswick) is made up of three reserves: Walberswick, Hen Reedbeds and Dingle Marshes. Walberswick's habitats include reed beds, hay meadows, grazing marshes and a variety of woodlands, while Hen Reedbed is a man-made mix of reed beds, fens, dykes and pools, which were created in 1999 by the Suffolk Wildlife Trust to provide new breeding habitats for bitterns and other wildlife. Other birdlife here includes marsh harriers, herons, bearded tits, and reed and sedge warblers, and in the evenings there is an astonishing display of up to 50,000 roosting starlings.

Dingle Marshes, near Leiston, is jointly owned and managed by the RSPB and the Suffolk Wildlife Trust. It attracts breeding and wintering wildfowl and waders, including avocets, white-fronted geese, lapwings and redshanks. The site is also home

1 The fast-eroding cliffs and coastline at Dunwich **2** Purple heather beside a path through Dunwich Heath **3** Avocet and chick at the Minsmere RSPB Reserve **4** Camouflaged oystercatcher eggs laid on the shingle of Orford Ness

to a significant proportion of the UK's marsh harrier and bittern populations. The Orfordness–Havergate NNR lies south of Aldeburgh, and consists of the largest vegetated shingle spit in the country, which gradually isolated the former port of Orford as it grew and diverted the River Alde southwards. The spit was formed by the deposition of shingle through wave action and longshore drift, an ongoing process, which means that the 10-mile (16km) long spit is still growing. The shingle supports a number of rare invertebrates – particularly beetles and spiders – and the site, an RSPB reserve, is also important for many breeding birds, including terns, avocets and short-eared owls.

Composers and pagodas

The low-lying coastal hinterland contains some of England's few remaining areas of ancient open heathland such as that at Dunwich Heath, which is the best surviving example of 'sandlings' – heathlands of heather and bracken – which were grazed by enormous flocks of sheep in medieval times. Today, they are the home of all three species of heather, gorse and broom, and the nationally rare nightjar, Dartford warbler, woodlark and antlion, and Britain's only poisonous snake, the adder. From July to September, the heath is awash with colour – a vivid patchwork of pink and purple heather and coconut-scented golden gorse.

Colourful pink- and yellow-washed cottages glow in the few towns and villages within the AONB. One of the most famous, Aldeburgh, was the home for many years of the controversial composer Benjamin Britten and his lifelong partner, the singer Peter Pears. Britten's masterpiece *Peter Grimes* (1945) was set in the area. Aldeburgh has a fine street of Georgian houses, while the Moot Hall on the seafront is a timber-framed building dating from the mid-17th century. It has been used for council meetings for over 400 years and still houses the Town Clerk's office and an interesting local museum.

Aldeburgh's wide shingle beach boasts the controversial sculpture *Scallop*, by local artist Maggi Hambling. The interlocking stainless-steel scallop shells are dedicated to Benjamin Britten, who loved to walk along the beach. People are encouraged to sit on the shells and watch the sea.

The former maltings at nearby Snape have been turned into a smart shopping outlet. A converted red-brick warehouse is used as the venue for the famous Aldeburgh Music Festival, founded by Britten and Pears in 1948, which takes place every June.

Orford is an even older settlement on the River Alde, cut off from the sea now by the shingle spit of Orford Ness but once an important medieval port. The splendidly preserved, polygonal three-turreted castle keep, which is owned by English Heritage, was built in 1165 by Henry II to control his East Anglian interests. It makes a fine viewpoint towards the red-and-white lighthouse and concrete 'pagodas' on Orford Ness.

The pagodas of Orford Ness are a chilling reminder of the Cold War. The Ministry of Defence conducted secret military tests here during both World Wars, as well as in the Cold War. The Atomic Weapons Research Establishment also had a base on the site, using it for the environmental testing of detonators and outer casings of nuclear weapons. The distinctive pagodas were designed to contain any accidental explosions. Orford Ness is now owned by the National Trust, but it can be visited by the ferry from Orford only on designated open days.

The town of Southwold, dominated by its somewhat incongruously sited white lighthouse tower in among its streets, and the village of Walberswick across the Blyth estuary have both enjoyed a new lease of life with the burgeoning tourist trade.

1 Maggi Hambling's *Scallop* sculpture on the beach at Aldeburgh **2** Colourful beach huts at Southwold, with the lighthouse behind **3** An aerial view of the 10-mile (16km) long shingle spit of Orford Ness

1

2

A TOWN BENEATH THE WAVES

The town of Dunwich, south of Southwold, was an important port in Saxon and Norman times, boasting a population of 5,000 and three churches. However, a fierce storm in 1328, which diverted the River Blyth northwards, effectively obliterated the settlement. The crashing North Sea breakers left only a couple of solitary gravestones from the former church of All Saints, near the cliff, and the crumbling archway and walls of the Greyfriars friary as the only evidence of the medieval town lost beneath the waves.

CANNOCK CHASE

Cannock Chase, a 27 square mile (68sq km) wilderness of heathland and forestry plantations, has always provided a valuable 'lung' for the people of the densely populated West Midlands and the Black Country. The AONB was designated in 1958 and covers the upland parts of mid-Staffordshire between Stafford, Rugeley, Burntwood and Cannock. Although one of the smallest mainland AONBs, it is also one of the most heavily used and threatened.

The name of Cannock Chase gives away its early history. The term 'chase' was used to describe an unenclosed area set aside for hunting in medieval times, and a large population of wild deer – red, fallow and roe – still inhabits the thickly regimented Forestry Commission plantations, which have largely replaced the ancient deciduous forest.

Within day-trip distance of three million people, Cannock Chase has long been an important recreational area. Today, the more enlightened policies of the Forestry Commission allow plentiful public access on waymarked paths and bridleways. The Commission has also instituted a regime for the conservation of the remaining patches of old oak woodland, such as that still found at Brocton Coppice in the northwest of the area, and the abundant wildlife, which includes adders and nightjars as well as deer.

Adders are Britain's commonest and only poisonous snake, distinguished from their harmless cousins the grass snake by their generally darker colour and the V-shaped patterning on their heads. They enjoy the dry and often sunny aspect of the Chase's heathlands, but are usually shy and nervous creatures and will not attack unless provoked.

The mysterious nocturnal nightjar, also known locally as the goat owl in the traditional belief that it takes milk from nanny goats during the night, has a weird, churring call, which adds to its mystique. It is a master of camouflage, and its beautiful marbled, grey-brown plumage makes it almost invisible when it is roosting during the day, and perfectly suited to the dry bracken and heaths of Cannock Chase.

In recognition of this rich wildlife, much of the Chase has also been designated a Site of Special Scientific Interest (SSSI), but in addition, 3,000 acres of the area are also one of Britain's largest country parks, run by Staffordshire County Council. Traffic-free roads, nature trails and a strong emphasis on conservation ensure that landscape and wildlife interests are protected.

1 Heathland and hills at Cannock Chase **2** Male red deer roaring during the annual rut **3** Male adder **4** Graves at the German Military Cemetery

1

2

A CORNER OF A FOREIGN FIELD

The sombre and moving German Military Cemetery (left) on Cannock Chase includes the graves of nearly 5,000 German servicemen who died in World Wars I and II.

In the main entrance and courtyard, a recumbent bronze sculpture represents The Fallen Warrior. The tombstones of black Belgian granite mark the fallen of both World Wars – a total of 2,143 from World War I, and 2,797 from World War II.

Opened in 1967, the cemetery was built by the German War Graves Commission. Whether they died as prisoners of war, were airmen who were shot down or crashed, or sailors who died at sea, the German dead were brought to Cannock as their final resting place. They include the crews of four Zeppelins, shot down over Britain during World War I. This melancholy place is visited by many relatives of those who rest here.

3

4

2

3

4

Upland nature

Apart from commercial forestry, other land uses in the AONB include sand and gravel extraction on the edges of the Chase, while a small part of it still remains in the hands of the Ministry of Defence as a firing range. The military use is well established here, and there are both German (see box) and Commonwealth cemeteries commemorating the dead of the two World Wars. For many British soldiers during World War I, Cannock was their last experience of England before leaving for Flanders and the horrors of the trenches.

Despite modern pressures, Cannock Chase remains a surprisingly wild area of heather-clad heathlands, birch and oak woodlands, and the more recent blanket conifer plantations. Many peaceful valleys dissect the forest, and the whole area is surrounded by the extensive landscaped parklands of great houses such as Shugborough Hall, the ancestral home of the Earls of Lichfield, which today is managed jointly by Staffordshire County Council and the National Trust.

Shugborough boasts that it is the UK's most complete working historic estate, and the magnificent landscape you see today is largely the work of Thomas Anson, who inherited the modest family seat from his father William in 1720. Thomas spent the next 50 years creating a lasting legacy of Georgian style and elegance, and a parkland full of rococo 'eye-catcher' monuments.

The central section of the mansion house itself was built in 1694 by William Anson, with the wings added in 1748. The back of the house – originally the front entrance – was extended between 1790 and 1806, and the 10-columned portico (the columns are, in fact, hollow) and steps were added as part of architect Samuel Wyatt's redevelopment. Inside, the house has an abundance of rich, rococo ornamentation, reflecting the wealth and importance of the Anson family.

But Shugborough is perhaps most famous for its grounds and the extensive model farm, which is still run as a working unit. The walled gardens, designed by Wyatt between 1805 and 1806, supplied the house with all the meat, vegetables, fruit and flowers it needed. The 1,000-acre parkland of Shugborough is dotted with an eccentric collection of follies and monuments, such as the Tower of the Winds, the Triumphal Arch and the Doric Temple, all of which are Grade I listed monuments.

The upland nature of the Chase had made it attractive to the earliest settlers, and one of the most important prehistoric sites is the Iron Age hillfort of Castle Ring, which lies to the south of Rugeley. At 800ft (244m), it is the highest point of the Chase. The 8-acre hillfort is built in the shape of a pentagon, with defences that vary with the topography of the hilltop. Castle Ring also enjoys wide views across the Chase and the Trent Valley.

1 Sunbeams shed a golden light over Fairoak Pools **2** Common blue damselflies bejewelled by dewdrops **3** Cyclists on the Route to Health through Cannock Chase **4** Clipped yews lead up through the gardens to the rear of Shugborough Hall

THE COTSWOLDS

The largest and probably the best known of England's AONBs, the Cotswold Hills are a gently undulating landscape founded on cream-coloured oolitic limestone, which presents a steep escarpment to the east of the valley of the River Severn.

Most people would agree that the Cotswolds epitomize the idyllic English landscape. Mellow, honey-stoned villages are watched over by superb, pinnacled churches, all sitting in chocolate-box perfection among green rolling hills. The name gives away the character of the region – they are the 'cotes', or sheep shelters, on the 'wolds', the gentle hills of Jurassic limestone that form the skeleton of the landscape.

Designated in 1966, the Cotswolds AONB covers 787 square miles (2,018sq km), which is larger than many national parks. The hills are threaded by the 100-mile (161km) Cotswold Way long-distance path, which follows the lip of the escarpment between Bath and Chipping Campden, while the Thames Path National Trail sets out from the river's source near Kemble on its 180-mile (290km) journey east to the Thames Barrier beyond the capital. In addition, a multitude of footpaths and bridleways makes it wonderful country to explore on foot, by bicycle or on horseback.

1 The pinnacled perpendicular tower of St James Church, Chipping Campden, a typical Cotswold 'wool' church. The Lodge stands on the left **2** Evening view towards North Nibley from Uley Bury

2

Lucrative wool trade

The Cotswolds are nationally important for their rare limestone grasslands, such as Cleeve Common above Cheltenham, and ancient, hanging beech woods. These include Cotswold Commons and Beechwoods National Nature Reserve (NNR) near Sheepscombe, where you will find the glorious beeches of Buckholt Wood, and Cranham and Edge Commons. They are also home to some national rarities, such as the large blue butterfly (see box), as well as rich flora on the upper slopes of most of the deeply incised valleys, or combes.

The land slopes away gently in a broad plateau from the escarpment edge, which looks over the Severn Valley and the Vale of Evesham. The plateau, crisscrossed by an intricate network of distinctive dry-stone walls, is split by deep valleys where villages built of the warm, honey-coloured stone have existed for centuries alongside the life-giving, crystal-clear limestone streams.

Many Cotswold villages, such as Chipping Campden and Winchcombe, have magnificent medieval churches, built with the wealth generated by the lucrative wool trade – the rich, soft wool of the large, curly-fleeced Cotswold sheep was a highly valued commodity throughout Europe during the Middle Ages. An ancient breed, the Cotswold sheep, with its grey or white face and well-developed woolly forelock, is a rare breed today but, in medieval times, when at its most popular, up to 5,000 rams were sold or let in a season. The breed has contributed to the formation of several others, including the Hampshire Down and Leicester sheep.

Venerated hills

The human history of the Cotswolds goes back much further than that of its sheep. Prehistoric monuments such as the impressive Neolithic long barrows of Belas Knap, near Winchcombe, and Nympsfield and Hetty Pegler's Tump, near Uley, show how these hills were venerated by the earliest 'Cotsallers', the affectionate name given to local residents.

At a height of 984ft (300m), the Belas Knap chambered long barrow is reached by a steep uphill path. With fine views of the surrounding Cotswold countryside, this impressive dry-stone monument is 164ft (50m) long and up to 59ft (18m) wide, and 13ft (4m) high at the broadest end. Inside, there are four small polygonal burial chambers, where excavations have revealed nearly 40 skeletons. It is thought that the skeletons may have been brought out for special occasions or rituals, to remind those present of their ancestors.

The grassy, 118ft (36m) long mound of Hetty Pegler's Tump ('tump' is the local word for a barrow) was named after the wife of a 17th-century landowner. At least 23 skeletons were found in the two internal chambers when they were excavated.

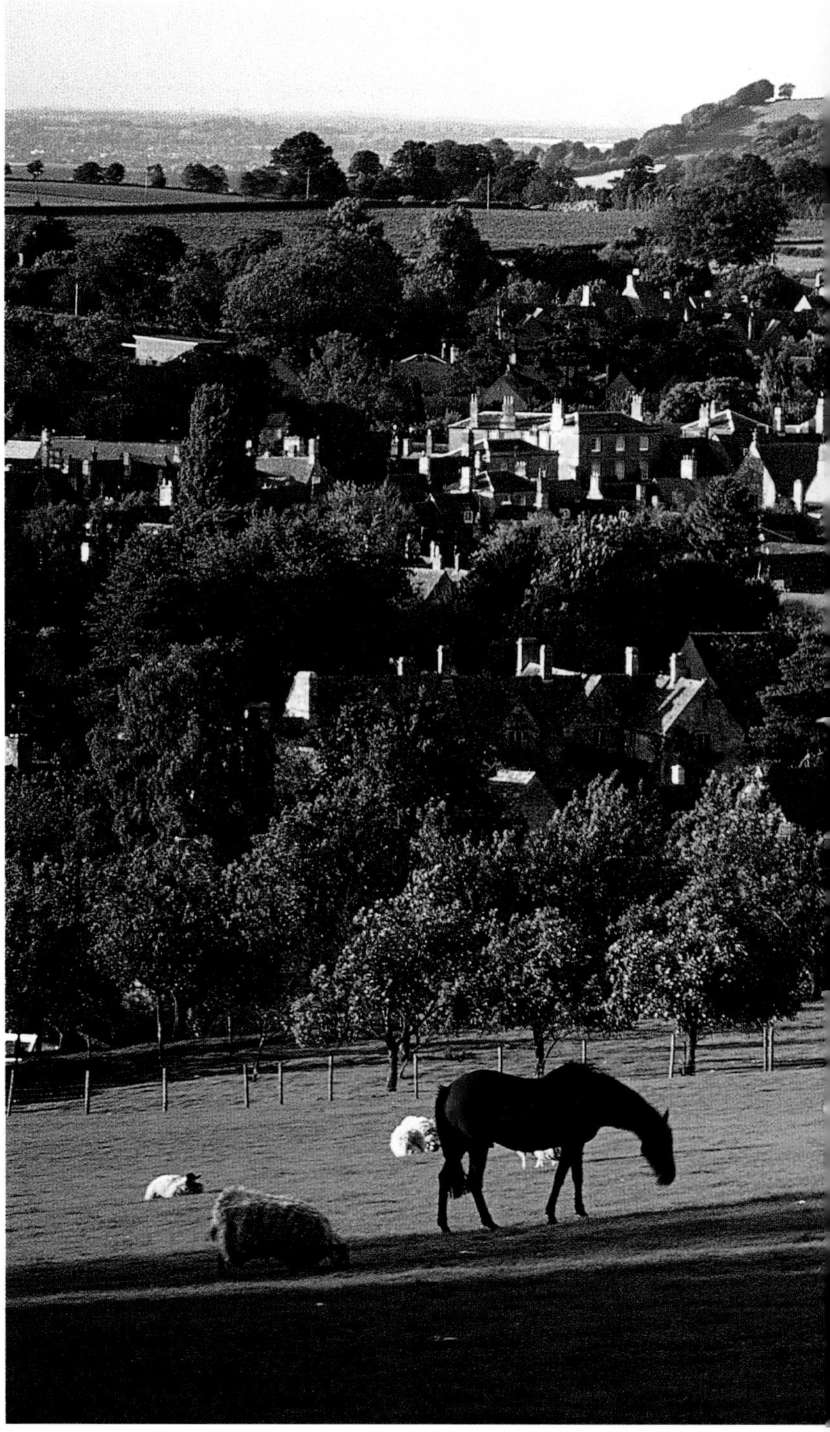
1

2

1 The rooftops of Chipping Campden, watched over by the tower of St James church **2** Nympsfield chambered long barrow dates from the Neolithic Age **3** A dry-stone wall in Sheep Street, Chipping Campden **4** Large blue butterfly

THE LARGE BLUE BUTTERFLY

The large blue butterfly (left), which was recently reintroduced to the Cotswolds by ecologists from Natural England, has a very strange lifecycle that was not fully understood until the 1970s.

After hatching from eggs, which are laid exclusively on wild thyme, the caterpillar of the large blue drops to the ground and secretes a tantalizing fluid that fools a certain species of red ant into believing it is an ant grub. The parasitic caterpillar is then picked up and taken to the safety of the ant nest, where it continues the pretence, sometimes by apparently 'singing' to the ants. It lives in the nest for most of the year, feeding off ant grubs, before emerging as a beautiful butterfly in June.

3

4

1

The Severn escarpment is also punctuated by a string of impressive Iron Age hillforts, the most notable of which are to be found at Uley Bury, Crickley Hill and Painswick Hill. Each commands extensive views across the valley of the River Severn, and as far as the Malvern Hills to the north.

Cirencester, a bustling market town situated halfway along the southern edge of the AONB, went by the name of Corinium Dobunnorum in Roman times. A major military centre as well as the Romans' regional capital, it later became the provincial capital and the second largest town in Roman Britain. Early in the occupation, the Romans subjugated the native population by imposing a military road system across the countryside, and three of their major highways – the Fosse Way, Akeman Street and Ermin Street – radiated out from Cirencester. Important Roman remains have been discovered in the town and at the many rich villa sites nearby, such as Chedworth, North Leigh and Great Witcombe, complete with mosaic flooring and central heating systems.

The Corinium Museum in Park Street, Cirencester, which has recently undergone a £5 million refurbishment, contains the finest collection of Roman artefacts to be found in the region, along with many other interesting exhibits. These include the reconstruction of the grave of 'Mrs Getty', a 6th-century Anglo-Saxon princess, so named because of the astonishing richness of the 500 grave goods buried with her.

There was also a Roman walled town at Dorn, near Moreton-in-Marsh, and two other substantial Roman settlements have been located on the Fosse Way at Bourton-on-the-Water and at Lower Slaughter. Another large town, with a regular layout of paved streets, has recently been uncovered at Wycombe, to the west of Bourton-on-the-Water.

Idyllic towns

The Cotswold countryside was evidently well settled and prosperous during Roman times. The villas in the north Cotswolds are generally not as elaborate or numerous as those farther to the south around Cirencester, although several have been found and excavated. Archaeologists now think that the villa estates must have been established within the existing Celtic pattern of rural life, because many enclosures recorded from aerial photographs represent settlements that were already part of a settled and well-populated landscape.

Agriculture, with sheep farming gradually being superseded by mixed and arable regimes, is still one of the most important industries in the Cotswolds. But tourism, with its associated service industries, is now the major employer of the 120,000 people who live within the AONB.

The Cotswolds have become both a national and international tourist destination, and idyllic towns and villages such as Stow-on-the-Wold, Bourton-on-the-Water, Bibury and Castle Combe can become stiflingly overcrowded in summer. Film buffs may recognize Castle Combe – often referred to as the prettiest village in England – as the setting for the fantasy adventure *Stardust* (2007) starring Sienna Miller and numerous other feature films.

Stow-on-the-Wold, an ancient, mainly 16th-century, wool town built of mellow Cotswold limestone, stands on a hilltop at about 800ft (240m) above sea level, where the Fosse Way intersects with five other routes, including the prehistoric Jurassic Way and Salt Way. Notable buildings include St Edward's parish church, built between the 11th and 15th centuries. Its 88ft (27m) high tower, completed in 1447, watches over the busy Market Square with its restored 15th-century Market Cross. The King's Arms in the Market Square, with an arch leading to the stables, is a good example of a coaching inn. Charles I stayed here on his way to the Battle of Naseby in 1645, and the inn featured as itself (that is, as the King's Arms) in the BBC TV production of Thomas Hardy's *The Mayor of Casterbridge*. The Royalist Hotel at the end of Digbeth Street is claimed to be the oldest inn in England.

The low-arched footbridges over the River Windrush in Bourton-on-the-Water have led to the village being given the rather grandiose title of the Venice of the Cotswolds, and it is yet another Cotswold village regularly voted as the prettiest. The famous model village in Rissington Road duplicates Bourton at a scale of one-ninth of the original, and is a firm favourite with children. The originally Norman parish church of St Lawrence at Bourton was extensively redesigned in 1784, when the tower was surmounted by a classical balustrade and dome.

1 The Market Hall at Chipping Campden **2** Mosaics at Chedworth Roman villa **3** The yew-enshrouded doorway to St Edward's church, Stow-on-the-Wold, has a fairytale aspect **4** Footbridges over the River Windrush in Bourton-on-the-Water

2

3

4

MALVERN HILLS

Seen from the M5 motorway or the Birmingham–Bristol railway line, the Malvern Hills present a dim blue outline to the west, a sinuous ridge of hills that looks far higher than it really is. In fact, a Himalayan mountaineer once described the hills as the nearest thing that Britain has to a complete, isolated mountain range.

The highest point of the Malvern Hills – the 1,394ft (425m) summit of the Worcestershire Beacon at their northern extremity – is a fine viewpoint, extending eastwards across the Severn plain and to the Cotswolds beyond, and westwards towards the blue first foothills of neighbouring Wales.

The Malverns really are a mountain range in miniature, a north–south ridge of ancient Precambrian rocks running for about 8 miles (13km) between the Severn Valley and the valleys of the Frome and Wye towards Wales. The hills also constitute some of the oldest rocks in Britain, formed by heavily folded and faulted Precambrian rocks from the very dawn of planet earth.

These hard, pastel-shaded rocks were in great demand for hardcore, and quarrying once threatened the distinctive skyline of the Malvern Hills. It was saved only by the formation of the Malvern Hills Conservators, an independent local authority founded in 1884 and one of Britain's earliest conservation bodies. The organization still manages most of this 40 square mile (105sq km) AONB, which was officially designated in 1959.

The landscape of the Malvern Hills ranges from the open grasslands and commons of the high ridge – the name comes from the Welsh *moel bryn*, or 'bare hill' – to the steep, limestone slopes of the western flanks, which support fine mixed stands of deciduous woodlands. In contrast, the lowland parts of the AONB consist of fertile sandstones and marls to the southeast. West of the hills, alternate beds of limestone and sandstone create a landscape of gentle scarps and valleys, with meadows, fields and orchards crossed by a network of narrow lanes.

Sinuous earthworks

The Malvern Hills have presented a natural barrier and border for much of their human history. Towards the southern end of the ridge, the great sinuous earthworks of the British Camp encircling the summit of Herefordshire Beacon mark one of the most spectacular and complete Iron Age hillforts in Britain. At its centre is the circular earthwork known as the Citadel, showing how the later Normans utilized the Iron Age defences as a motte and bailey castle. Another hillfort commanding the southern end of the ridge is found at Midsummer Hill, near Hollybush.

Right Looking north towards the Worcestershire Beacon from the Herefordshire Beacon, or British Camp, which stands at the mid-point of the Malvern Hills ridge

1

2

3

4

The central spine of the Malvern ridge is traversed by the Shire Ditch, or Red Earl's Dyke, which was constructed by Gilbert de Clare, the eponymous red-haired Earl of Gloucester, in the 13th century. The earthwork still effectively marks the boundary between the old counties of Worcestershire and Herefordshire for much of its length.

Inspiring landscape

The more recent history of the Malvern Hills has been dominated by the growth of Great Malvern and Malvern Wells as a health spa (see box). Tourists have flocked here since the early 1800s to 'take the waters' at places such as St Ann's Well, Malvern's most famous spring of pure water, on the hills above Great Malvern. It was at the height of its fame as a spa that the engineered paths, which are such a feature of the walks across and around the hills, were laid down. Malvern retained its popularity as a Victorian pleasure garden, and today it is still popular as a day-trip destination for thousands of people from the West Midlands.

Originally a Benedictine monastery dating from 1085, the priory at Great Malvern now serves as the parish church of St Mary and St Michael. Perpendicular-style additions to the original Norman church began in around 1440 and continued until 1502. The great central tower is very similar to that of nearby Gloucester Cathedral, giving rise to the suggestion that it probably had the same architect and was built by the same masons. In the chancel is the monument to John Knotsford, who died in 1589 and who supervised the dissolution of the former monastery. It is largely due to Knotsford that the church, and particularly its fine display of medieval glass, survived.

Malvern Priory is famous for its fine collection of stained glass, ranging from medieval to modern, and including windows from the 15th to the 19th centuries. The north transept window, depicting the coronation of St Mary, was a gift from Henry VII in 1501. The Duke of Gloucester, later Richard III, donated another. Restoration of the priory was carried out in 1860 under the direction of Sir George Gilbert Scott, who designed the roof of the nave in imitation of the medieval original.

The Malvern Hills have inspired artists for generations, none more so than the celebrated English composer Sir Edward Elgar, who was born in their shadow at Lower Broadheath in 1857. He is said to have based his cantata *Caractacus* on the site of one of the British leader's legendary last stands against the Romans, which took place at the British Camp on Herefordshire Beacon. Elgar's daughter, Carice Irene (1890–1970), once explained in an interview: 'No one was more imbued with his own countryside than my father.'

1 St Ann's Well, Malvern's best-known natural spring **2** Stained glass depicting Queen Victoria with her grandson, Kaiser Wilhelm II of Germany, in the north aisle of Great Malvern Priory, given to celebrate her Golden Jubilee in 1887 **3** Statue of Sir Edward Elgar at Great Malvern **4** Great Malvern Priory in frosty conditions **5** Malvern water gushes from a spring in the hills

5

MALVERN WATER

There are about 70 natural springs around the Malvern Hills, each releasing an average of about 60 litres of fresh water every minute, and the flow never ceases. The water is famous for its purity, but when Dr John Wall tested it in 1756, it led 18th-century wits to summarize his findings in this well-known couplet:

The Malvern water, says Doctor John Wall,
Is famed for containing just nothing at all.

The town developed massively in the Victorian era when 'taking the waters' became fashionable. A key date was 1842, when Dr James Manby Gully and Dr James Wilson set up their water cure establishments in Belle Vue in the centre of town, where they treated such illustrious 19th-century figures as Charles Darwin and Charles Dickens.

The water has been bottled commercially at Colwall under the Schweppes brand since 1850, and on a smaller scale as Holywell Spring Water by a family-owned company since 2009. Apparently, Queen Victoria would never travel without her Malvern water, and neither will Elizabeth II.

A WORCESTERSHIRE LAD

Despite his most famous collection of poems being about the Shropshire Hills, Alfred Edward Housman had not even visited the county when he wrote it.

Housman (right) was born in 1859 in Fockbury, Worcestershire, one of seven children whose father was a solicitor. Housman was extremely close to his mother, and her death on his 12th birthday was a cruel blow, which is thought to be the reason for the overriding pessimism expressed in his poetry. Apparently convinced that he must never find love, Housman became increasingly reclusive and turned to his notebooks for solace, where he had begun to write the poems that eventually made up *A Shropshire Lad,* which was first published in 1896.

He assumed the unlikely role of farm labourer in the poems, and set them in the 'blue remembered hills' of Shropshire, a county that had always figured on his distant horizon. Sales of *A Shropshire Lad* grew slowly, but as they did Housman's popularity increased, so that by the time his *Last Poems* were published in 1922, he was enjoying great literary success.

2

3

1

4

SHROPSHIRE HILLS

Into my heart an air that kills
From yon far country blows:
What are those blue remembered hills,
What spires, what farms are those?

From *A Shropshire Lad* (1896) by A E Housman (1859–1936)

'Those blue remembered hills' described by Housman (see box) are the Shropshire Hills, a landscape of looming bare ridges and lush pastoral farms on the borders of England and Wales and crossed by the Dark Age boundary of Offa's Dyke.

Designated in 1958, the Shropshire Hills AONB covers 310 square miles (804sq km) of a landscape dotted with hillforts and other fortifications, evidence of how the area has been disputed and fought over for generations.

The most prominent physical features are the hills themselves, ranging from the vast Precambrian whaleback moorland of the Long Mynd to the weird, shattered quartzite of the Stiperstones, and the limestone ridge of Wenlock Edge, near Much Wenlock. The highest hills are the Clee Hills, made of sandstone with a capping of basalt, which have attracted both coal miners and quarrymen over the years.

The highest point is Brown Clee Hill at 1,788ft (545m), although Titterstone Clee and Catherton Common, on the bleak high point of the Kidderminster–Ludlow road, are not much lower. This varied geology gives rise to a fascinating landscape of parallel ridges and valleys, generally running in a northeast to southwest direction.

There are five distinct upland areas in the Shropshire Hills AONB: the Long Mynd and Stiperstones above Church Stretton; Clun Forest; the Clee Hills; Hopesay Hill; and the hillfort-topped, isolated volcanic outlier of the Wrekin, which towers above the modern overspill town of Telford. 'To all friends round the Wrekin' is still a rousing toast heard in Shropshire.

The extensive areas of open common land in this AONB serve as important upland habitats in the generally low-lying Midlands. For that reason, the Stiperstones ridge, capped by the mysterious outcrop of the Devil's Chair, a quartzite tor surrounded by heather and bilberry moorland, is a National Nature Reserve (NNR). The legend that inspired the name is that the Devil dropped an apronful of stones on the summit, which he had intended to use to fill Hell Gutter, a steep ravine on the slopes of the hill. Apparently, if you sit in the 'chair' at midnight on the longest day of the year, the Devil himself will reappear. Local novelist Mary Webb described the

1 Late evening sun lights the heather on the Long Mynd in this view towards the Carding Mill Valley **2** Alfred Edward Housman **3** A fruiting head of cotton grass **4** The bubbling stream in the Carding Mill Valley

1

2

3

Stiperstones as the Diafol (or Devil's) Mountain in her best-known novel, *The Golden Arrow* (1916). 'It drew the thunder, people said. Storms broke suddenly round it out of a clear sky. No one cared to cross the range near it after dark… it remained inviolable, taciturn, evil.' Even today, Natural England's website warns that the ridge is subject to lightning strikes.

Legendary sites

The Long Mynd, a vast plateau of heather and bilberry moorland, is now managed for wildlife conservation and the raising of red grouse. From its highest point at 1,696ft (517m), it is possible to see as far as the Cheshire plain, and the Brecon Beacons and Cadair Idris in South Wales.

The Midland Gliding Club, which occupies a 331-acre site at the southern end of the Mynd, is one of the oldest gliding clubs in the UK. Gliding started here in the 1930s, and one of the club's first members was the pioneering female aviator Amy Johnson.

Human settlement began early in the Shropshire Hills, and there is a fine collection of Iron Age hillforts, such as that which crowns the Wrekin; on Caer Caradoc near Church Stretton, another of the legendary sites of the last stand of Caractacus against the Romans (a legend it shares with the British Camp on Herefordshire Beacon in the Malvern Hills); Croft Ambrey, southwest of Ludlow; and on Bodbury Hill, flanking the Carding Mill Valley, the most popular point of access to the Long Mynd. The Mynd itself (the name reflects this country's border nature, and comes from the Welsh for mountain) is crossed by a prehistoric track known as the Portway, and is punctuated by a number of Bronze Age barrows.

Offa's Dyke, the 8th-century boundary constructed by King Offa of the Mercians to mark his western boundary with Wales, runs north–south through the area and is followed by the 168-mile (270km) Offa's Dyke National Trail, opened by Everest conqueror Sir John Hunt in his home town of Knighton in 1971. The 35-mile (56km) Six Shropshire Summits challenge walk, the brainchild of Birmingham journalist and writer Vivian Bird, takes in all the Shropshire hills over 1,500ft (457m), namely Titterstone Clee, Brown Clee, Caer Caradoc, the Long Mynd, the Stiperstones and Corndon Hill.

Most of the larger towns of this part of Shropshire are excluded from the AONB. The largest settlements are Church Stretton, nestling at the mouth of the beautiful Carding Mill Valley to the east of the Long Mynd; Craven Arms, with its famous sheep market; and the sleepy little black-and-white half-timbered township of Clun. The troubled past of the region is highlighted by the number of castles and fortified houses, such as those at Clun and Stokesay, and Roger Montgomery's great red sandstone castle at nearby Ludlow, built to hold back the unconquered Welsh.

1 The luscious berries of the bilberry **2** The Midland Gliding Club flies from Asterton, on the western edge of the Long Mynd **3** The half-timbered gatehouse to Stokesay Castle **4** The jagged quartzite rocks of the Stiperstones

WYE VALLEY

The Wye Valley is one of England's best-loved landscapes, where the River Wye winds through wooded gorges and rich water meadows, and past such notable landmarks as Tintern Abbey, Symonds Yat and Chepstow Castle, before reaching the mighty Severn estuary.

The great, looping incised meander of the River Wye at Symonds Yat in Herefordshire is one of the showplaces of British topography. It was formed comparatively recently in geological terms, during the Pleistocene period about two million years ago, when the sea level dropped and the land was suddenly uplifted. The limestone rocks were cut through by the Wye, as a knife cuts through butter.

The steep, wooded cliffs, formerly inhabited by Stone Age man at Arthur's and Merlin's Caves and the site of an Iron Age hillfort on the summit of Yat Rock, are now once again the home of that elegant raptor, the peregrine falcon, which would have been a common sight to those earlier settlers.

Symonds Yat (its name comes from *yat*, which is the Old English for gate) is, however, only one of many highlights in this linear AONB, designated in 1971 and covering 126 square miles (326sq km) of Gloucestershire, Gwent, and Hereford and Worcester between Hereford and Chepstow. Others include the ruins of Tintern Abbey, founded by Cistercian monks in the 12th century and made famous by William Wordsworth's poem of the same name. Wordsworth was revisiting the Wye Valley in 1798 after an absence of five years when he wrote this poem, which is more about the surrounding valley than the ruins.

Suppressed by Henry VIII in 1536, Tintern Abbey is one of the most romantically situated monastic ruins in Britain. Now cared for by Cadw, it was founded by Walter de Clare, lord of nearby Chepstow, in 1131 as only the second Cistercian abbey in Britain. The abbey is claimed to be the first place in Britain where brass was made, and the entrepreneurial monks were also early iron-founders, using ore and charcoal from the nearby Forest of Dean.

Troubled history

High on a rocky crag overlooking the Wye, the buttressed Goodrich Castle, owned by English Heritage, was built and modified during the 12th and 13th centuries as a defence against the raiding Welsh. Originally an earth and wooden fortification, this was replaced in the middle of the 12th century by a light grey sandstone keep, which is still there, making a striking contrast with the deep red towers, gatehouse and curtain walls added in the late 13th century.

1 The elegant peregrine falcon has returned to its former haunt at Symonds Yat **2** The purple hoods of foxglove **3** A corner of Tintern Abbey **4** The incised meander of the River Wye seen from Yat Rock

1

2

3

4

1

THE MAN OF ROSS

A philanthropist and benefactor, John Kyrle (right) was a prominent figure in 18th-century Ross-on-Wye. Famously the subject of a poem by Alexander Pope, Kyrle assisted the rector in his parish work and distributed bread to the poor. 'He had not been born the Earl of Ross, the Baron of Ross, the Knight of Ross, but he had made himself the Man of Ross,' it was claimed in St Mary's parish magazine of November 1893.

Kyrle's unblemished memory is still honoured in the town in one of its most notable inns, The Man of Ross, as well as in the John Kyrle High School.

2

3

4

Goodrich Castle was the seat of the powerful Talbot family, before it fell into disrepair in late Tudor times. As well as commanding an important crossing of the River Walesford, also known as Walford, it also guards the line of the former Roman road from Gloucester to Caerleon as it crosses from England into Wales.

Chepstow's great Norman castle, now in the hands of Cadw, stands on a cliff overlooking the River Wye, and is claimed to be the oldest surviving stone fortification in Britain. It was built from 1067 by the Norman Lord William FitzOsbern, who later became Earl of Hereford, and was the southernmost in the chain of castles constructed along the English–Welsh border. Monmouth's fortified 13th-century Monnow Bridge is further evidence of the troubled history of this disputed borderland.

There is even earlier evidence of this land being fought over. The still-impressive remains of Offa's Dyke, the 8th-century embanked earthwork built by King Offa of the Mercians, runs the length of the AONB and is followed by the 168-mile (270km) Offa's Dyke National Trail. Another Iron Age hillfort is hidden among the trees of Chase Wood, north of Goodrich and just south of Ross-on-Wye.

The Wye was the first major river in Britain to be designated a Site of Special Scientific Interest (SSSI) for its entire length, a rare accolade made in recognition of its high value to wildlife. It is renowned as a refuge for rare species like otters and the Symonds Yat peregrines, and as one of the last remaining large tracts of ancient limestone, broadleaved woodlands. The AONB's farmed landscapes are also rich natural habitats.

The main market town within the AONB is Ross-on-Wye, which clusters its Tudor and Georgian buildings around a great horseshoe bend in the Wye, overlooked by the elegant 14th-century spire of St Mary's parish church. Regular markets are still held around the 17th-century red sandstone Market House in the town centre, where the upper storey now houses a heritage centre.

Ross lays claim to being the birthplace of the British tourism industry. As early as 1745, Dr John Egerton, a rector, started taking friends on boat trips down the valley from his rectory at Ross. The Wye Valley's beautiful riverside scenery, precipitous cliffs and castles and abbeys were perfectly suited to the new picturesque fashion of landscape appreciation, and, in 1782, William Gilpin's book *Observations on the River Wye* became the first illustrated tour guide to be published in Britain. Other guides soon followed and Ross quickly became a centre for exploring the Wye.

Around two million visits each year are now made to the Wye Valley, with motorways making it easily accessible from the Midlands, Bristol and South Wales. The Wye is a major salmon-fishing river and also very popular for water sports, particularly canoeing. In addition to Offa's Dyke National Trail, the waymarked 34-mile (55km) Wye Valley Walk is a favourite among ramblers.

1 The view over the River Wye from Goodrich Castle **2** Plaque on John Kyrle's House in Ross-on-Wye **3** Gnarled trees sprout from the rocks on the Wye Valley Walk north of Chepstow **4** Ross-on-Wye seen across the river at dusk, with the spire of St Mary's church on the skyline

ARNSIDE & SILVERDALE

Silvery-grey limestone hills, glistening sandbanks, salt marshes and ancient woodlands characterize this beautiful area, famous for its wonderful views across Morecambe Bay towards the distant blue hills of the Lake District.

The Arnside and Silverdale AONB covers 28 square miles (73sq km) and was designated in 1972. Situated at the northeast corner of Morecambe Bay and adjoining the southeast corner of the Lake District, this small but fascinating area offers an assortment of scenic contrasts. These range from the shifting sands of the great 'wet Sahara' of Morecambe Bay to the reed and willow marshes of Leighton Moss and the bare limestone crags and contorted pavements around the 522ft (159m) high point of Arnside Knott.

Sheltered by the Lake District hills from the prevailing westerly winds, Arnside and Silverdale in the southeast of Cumbria are noticeably milder than the surrounding uplands. When the hills of the Lake District are shrouded in cloud and mist, this area is often in bright sunlight. Such a microclimate, together with the varied geology of the area, has created a diverse vegetation that is rare in this part of the country.

In many ways, the Arnside and Silverdale AONB represents a microcosm of the landscape of northern England. The pattern of reclaimed mosses at the edge of the Kent estuary, the hedges or dry-stone walls of the unimproved pastureland around Arnside Knott, and ancient woodlands and copses all make up a uniquely varied habitat, which supports a wide range of wildlife.

In recognition of this wonderful diversity, large areas of the AONB are owned or managed by the National Trust, Natural England, the RSPB or local wildlife trusts. The unimproved limestone pastures around the exposed scars and pavements of limestone encircling Arnside Knott are rich in rare wildflowers, such as orchids, and at a secret location near the Gait Barrows National Nature Reserve (NNR), there is a thriving colony of Britain's rarest orchid, the showy maroon and yellow lady's slipper. The area also supports a large population of butterflies in the summer, including the bronze-winged, high brown fritillary, which has its national stronghold here, and the Duke of Burgundy fritillary.

The National Trust's beautifully managed semi-natural Eaves Wood near Silverdale, with its stately beeches and ancient yews, gives tantalizing glimpses of Morecambe Bay. From its highest point at the Jubilee 'Pepperpot' monument, you can even see Blackpool Tower far to the south.

Left The breathtaking view from Arnside Knott over the Kent estuary, with its railway viaduct, towards Whitbarrow and the Lakeland Fells

Nearby, up an abandoned rail incline, is Trowbarrow Quarry, famous for its rich collection of Carboniferous limestone fossils, which range from wheel-like colonial corals to a limestone pavement turned up onto its side to form a vertical cliff face. Trowbarrow is named after the distinctive 33ft (10m) wide feature known as the Trough, which formed between Leighton Moss and Sandside when the Woodbine shale eroded away between walls of more resistant Urswick limestone.

Other paths lead from Silverdale down to the limestone headland of Jenny Brown's Point, where copper was smelted and exported in the 18th century. Jenny Brown was, apparently, a children's nanny who was drowned in the fast-rising waters of Morecambe Bay while attempting to save her charges.

The RSPB's famous reserve at Leighton Moss, established in 1964, is one of the last places in Britain where the unique booming 'whoomp!' call of the bittern, a shy, heron-like hunter of the marshes, can still be heard. The swaying reed beds are also home to the dashingly moustached bearded tits, which alight obligingly on specially prepared grit trays in the autumn. Other Leighton Moss birds include reed buntings and the graceful hovering marsh harrier, which can be watched in comfort from a series of hides, one of which (Lilian's Hide) is even carpeted! In autumn and winter, the reed beds are home to thousands of roosting starlings, which darken the sky with their 'murmurations'.

Leighton Moss is also one of the last British strongholds of the otter, and a well-developed system of paths and hides allows the visitor to see and learn about the fascinating range of wildlife.

Wintering wildfowl

The AONB extends well out onto the treacherous sands of Morecambe Bay, the most important estuary in Britain for its seabird and wildfowl populations. It has the third largest number of wintering wildfowl in the country, estimated at, on average, nearly 225,000 wintering wildfowl and 20,000 breeding sea birds. These include large populations of oystercatcher, knot, dunlin, curlew, pink-footed goose, shelduck and bar-tailed godwit, among many others. A tidal barrage scheme, which would have drained this wet wilderness, was abandoned in the 1990s after national protests at the possible loss of such an important wildlife habitat.

One of the great experiences to be enjoyed in the AONB is to take the 6-mile (10km) walk across the shifting sands from Hest Bank to Kents Bank on the Cumbrian shore. This should be done only in the company of the Queen's Guide to the Sands (see box).

The bay is crossed by the Furness railway (Lancaster to Barrow) route on the Arnside viaduct. The stations at Silverdale and Arnside are unmanned, but Carnforth station is forever linked with the 1945 David Lean film classic *Brief Encounter.*

1 A flock of oystercatchers rise from the Leighton Moss RSPB Reserve **2** Limestone pavement at Gait Barrows National Nature Reserve **3** Lady's slipper orchid in flower **4** An abandoned car partially buried in the treacherous sands at Morecambe Bay

1

2

THE QUEEN'S GUIDE TO THE SANDS

Cedric Robinson has been the Queen's Guide to the Sands for nearly half a century, during which time he has guided about half a million people across the sands of Morecambe Bay. The guide is an ancient post established in 1548, for which Cedric earns the princely annual sum of £15.

Bay crossers have included people as diverse as the Duke of Edinburgh (in a pony and trap), numerous television and show business personalities and literally thousands of ordinary people, many of whom have raised millions of pounds for charities to do what must be one of the most unusual walks in Britain.

Before he sets out on any walk, Cedric carefully reconnoitres the route, which changes daily with the shifting tides and quicksands, marking it out with what he calls 'brobs' – leaved branches of laurel. The route must at some stage cross the River Kent, which flows out into the bay – so wet feet are always to be expected.

As the incoming tide at Morecambe Bay is said to be able to outrun a galloping horse, and the quicksands have been known to swallow a Land Rover, it is as well to stick close to Cedric if you attempt the crossing.

3

4

1

FOREST OF BOWLAND

The beautiful Forest of Bowland is often overlooked by holidaymakers speeding north on the M6 towards the greater hills of the Lake District and Scotland.

Lying just to the east of the motorway and neatly demarcated by the river valleys of the Ribble, Lune and Wenning, which separate it from the Yorkshire Dales and the rest of the Pennines, the Forest of Bowland has always been a place apart. This sense of isolation and mystery is furthered by the fact that it is crossed by only one major road, through the famous Trough of Bowland. The forest is a little-known treasure, a wild and isolated place yet close to the large conurbations of northern England.

The Forest of Bowland AONB covers 310 square miles (802sq km) and was designated, along with neighbouring Pendle Hill, in 1963. An outlier of the Pennines, the forest is dominated by its central upland core of Carboniferous millstone grit fells, which are deeply incised by the river valleys of the Hodder, Wyre and Hindburn. Pendle Hill is a similar formation, separated from the forest by the River Ribble. The highest point of the Forest of Bowland is Ward's Stone, which rises to 1,837ft (560m), but much of the rest of the area is over 1,475ft (450m) above sea level.

It was the medieval period that had the greatest impact on the Bowland landscape. During this time, the royal hunting forests of Bowland were established – the title 'forest' referred to hunting rights, not to a large expanse of woodland, as we now interpret it. Except for the conifer plantations around the Stocks Reservoir near Tosside, there are actually very few trees in this heather-dominated, peaty moorland block today.

The king used his forest rights to prevent landowners from clearing and cultivating the land, restricting development and prohibiting change. This controlling influence continued long after the forest laws were revoked in 1507, as deer parks and smaller estates replaced the hunting forests.

Managing the landscape for game, primarily for grouse shooting, remains the predominant occupation today, and large private landowners, such as the Duchy of Lancaster, the Duke of Westminster and Lord Clitheroe, still own much of the Forest of Bowland. The largest owner is currently United Utilities water company, which manages a large area of the fells primarily for water catchment, and has introduced management policies designed to protect the area's rarer wildlife.

1 Undulating road through the Trough of Bowland **2** Cottages at Dunsop Bridge **3** Sunlight attempts to penetrate dense conifer forest on Beacon Fell **4** Sheep grazing on farmland in the Forest of Bowland

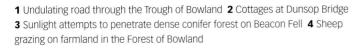

2

3

4

Bend in a river

Important mixed woodlands remain in the foothills, where the rich green of the river valleys is punctuated by solid, stone-built farms enclosed by miles of dry-stone walls and scattered but pretty gritstone villages such as Slaidburn and Newton. Slaidburn is the eastern terminus of the wild Trough of Bowland pass, the main road through the forest between Lancaster and Yorkshire. The total population of the area is 13,500.

The well-managed upland moors of Bowland, mainly used for sheep- and grouse-rearing, make them a nationally important area for nature conservation. Thirteen per cent of the area is designated as Sites of Special Scientific Interest (SSSIs), primarily for their important bird populations of curlew, golden plover, merlin and hen harrier, upland birds that are decreasing nationally.

Pendle Hill, the 1,831ft (558m) summit that dominates Clitheroe and Burnley to the southeast of the forest, is famous for its witch trials of the early 17th century (see box). But Pendle is known not only for devil worship. The summit was also the place in 1652 where the pioneer Quaker George Fox, 'moved of ye Lorde to goe atoppe of it', had the vision that led him to create the Society of Friends – the Quakers. 'I was moved to sounde ye day of ye Lorde & ye Lorde lett mee see a top of ye hill In what places hee had a great people,' he later wrote.

It was Bronze Age settlers who first cleared trees from the fells and began cultivating the land. They left little evidence of their presence, but the fells have remained largely clear of trees ever since. The Romans left behind two key routes through Bowland, the north–south Ribchester to Carlisle road, and a lesser east–west route, which is evident north of Downham.

The Norse settlers left their mark on our language as well as the landscape – for example, 'Pen' in Pendle means hill in Old Norse. Contrary to popular belief, the origins of the name Bowland have nothing to do with archery ('the land of the bow') or with medieval vaccaries (stock farms) – *bu* is Old Norse for cow. The name derives from the Old English *boga* or the Old Norse *bogi*, meaning a 'bow or bend in a river', and was probably coined in the 10th century to describe the topography of the Hodder basin, with its meandering river and streams.

Throughout Bowland there are many fine examples of 16th- to 18th-century stone buildings, with their characteristic stone mullions, lintels and date stones. There are also isolated reminders of the medieval heritage of the forest, for example the ruins of the Cistercian monastery at Sawley.

It has been estimated that a million people, mainly in the cities and towns of East Lancashire, live within a 30-minute car journey of the Forest of Bowland AONB. But, still, it manages to retain its sense of isolation and upland grandeur.

1

2

1 View along the winding River Hodder **2** Walkers approaching the trig point on the summit of Pendle Hill **3** Old Chattox, astride her broomstick, heads for Pendle Hill in this 1612 engraving **4** Golden plover in breeding plumage

THE PENDLE WITCHES

Tales of Old Mother Demdike, Old Chattox and Alice Nutter, popularized in William Harrison Ainsworth's melodramatic Victorian novel *The Lancashire Witches* (1849), still haunt the Pendle area.

The Pendle witches have provided the inspiration for the area's tourism, with local shops selling a variety of gifts with a witchcraft theme. There is even a local beer called Pendle Witches Brew, and a 45-mile (72km) footpath called the Pendle Way, waymarked by witches on broomsticks, which runs from the Pendle Heritage Centre at Barrowford to Lancaster Castle, where the accused witches were held before their trial.

Three generations of witches were said to be operating in the Pendle area in the early 17th century, led by Old Mother Demdike, who lived at the now-demolished Malkin Tower near Newchurch. As a result of the anti-Catholic and anti-witchcraft stance of James I, a total of 19 local women were arrested and charged with witchcraft, even though they were probably not guilty of anything more than a little eccentricity. Ten in all were sent to the gallows at York and Lancaster in 1612.

3

4

NIDDERDALE

Nidderdale is the Yorkshire Dales in microcosm. It has all the features of the rest of the Dales, from high, bleak moorland through to rich wooded valleys, overlaid by a rich legacy of history.

Nidderdale was apparently excluded from the Yorkshire Dales National Park when it was founded in 1954 because of the existence of the three reservoirs that flood its upper reaches. But the Gouthwaite, Angram and Scar House reservoirs, built between 1893 and 1936 to supply fresh water to Bradford and the towns of the West Riding, have weathered in to become essential softening elements in the landscape, and few visitors would object to their presence today.

Apart from the reservoirs, Nidderdale has numerous natural attractions, ranging from the wide, open moorlands of Great Whernside at the head of the dale to the amazing natural sculpture park of Brimham Rocks, near Pateley Bridge, and the wonderful limestone gorge of How Stean, near Middlesmoor. Just outside the dale in the valley of the River Skell, but included in the AONB, is the World Heritage Site of Fountains Abbey, perhaps the finest monastic ruin in Europe.

Special protection was proposed for Nidderdale as early as 1945, but it was not made an AONB until 1992. Covering 233 square miles (603sq km) of the eastern flanks of the Yorkshire Dales, the Nidderdale AONB includes the wooded dales of the rivers Washburn, Laver, Burn and Skell, as well as the Nidd itself.

The landscape is dominated by the millstone grit heather moorlands and acidic grasslands at the top of the dale, where the three reservoirs that flood the upper valley were constructed. The surrounding brooding hills of Great Whernside, Little Whernside and Hambleton Hill, which enclose the head of the valley, are vast and lonely sheep pastures, as well as the home of moorland-loving birds like the curlew and dunlin.

Limestone outcrops lower down the dale. The How Stean Gorge is a spectacular example of an 'active' limestone gorge (that is, a stream still runs through it), with the How Stean Beck flowing noisily below the elevated pathways that thread it. The scenery of How Stean is so out of this world that it was once used in an episode of BBC television's sci-fi classic *Doctor Who.* Elsewhere, the streams disappear underground in potholes such as Goyden Pot and Manchester Hole, near Middlesmoor.

There are also impressive public show caves at Stump Cross Caverns, originally discovered by local lead miners, on Greenhow Hill between Pateley Bridge and Grassington.

Left A typical Pennine farm is bathed in the golden light of dawn in this view near Greenhow Hill, west of Pateley Bridge

1

2

Scenic wonders

Perhaps the most famous scenic wonder of Nidderdale is a few miles south of the town of Pateley Bridge at Brimham Rocks. Probably the finest example of wind- and frost-eroded gritstone tors in Britain, the rocks are a fantastic collection of weird and wonderful shapes carved by the elements over countless aeons.

The fantastic rock architecture of Brimham was caused by differential erosion on the hard gritstone rocks, which were laid down in the Carboniferous period around 300 million years ago. The finishing touches were made by the timeless and persistent erosive forces of ice, wind and rain, to create the wonderful natural sculpture park that is the Brimham we see today.

Among the many named rock features at Brimham are the Druid's Idol, a massive 200-ton rock precariously perched on a pedestal only 12in (30cm) in diameter; the Druid's Writing Desk; the lifelike Dancing Bear; the Cannon; the Watchdog; and the Sphinx. The White Rocking Stone, high on the southern range of crags, received its name because it was once whitewashed and could be seen from Harrogate, nearly 10 miles (16km) away.

Much of Nidderdale was owned and managed in the Middle Ages as a huge sheep ranch by the Cistercian monks of Fountains Abbey in the valley of the River Skell to the east. This superb site formed part of the Marquess of Ripon's Studley Royal estate, and the grounds, including the magnificent ruins of the abbey, were landscaped by William Aislabie in the 18th century.

Fountains Abbey was founded in 1132 by Archbishop Thurstan of York, who brought a small group of 13 expelled monks from St Mary's Abbey in York to Herleshowe Wood in the wild and uninhabited valley of the River Skell to establish the monastery. According to later chronicles, it was 'a place remote from all the world… a wild and inhospitable place, more fitting to be the lair of wild beasts than of men.' The first monastery built by Thurstan and his monks was made of wood. Despite its remoteness, the monks had all they needed: shelter from the harsh northern weather, stone and wood for building, and a supply of running water.

From these humble beginnings grew the great Cistercian abbey of Fountains, one of the most important and powerful monastic sites in Europe. Most of the magnificent buildings we see today, including the stately 170ft (52m) high bell tower, were built by Abbot Marmaduke Huby in the late 15th century. Together with the Aislabie family's landscaped gardens of Studley Royal, Fountains Abbey became one of the first British World Heritage Sites in 1986.

Attractive stone-built villages such as Lofthouse, Middlesmoor, Ramsgill, Kirkby Malzeard and Pateley Bridge, the 'capital' of the dale and home of a famous agricultural show in September, make Nidderdale still a working, farming dale. However, as elsewhere, tourism is becoming increasingly important.

1 Druid's Idol, 200 tons balanced on a tiny plinth, Brimham Rocks **2** The other-worldly How Stean Gorge **3** The magnificent vaulted cellarium at Fountains Abbey **4** Grasses growing at Brimham Rocks **5** Green Man at Fountains Abbey

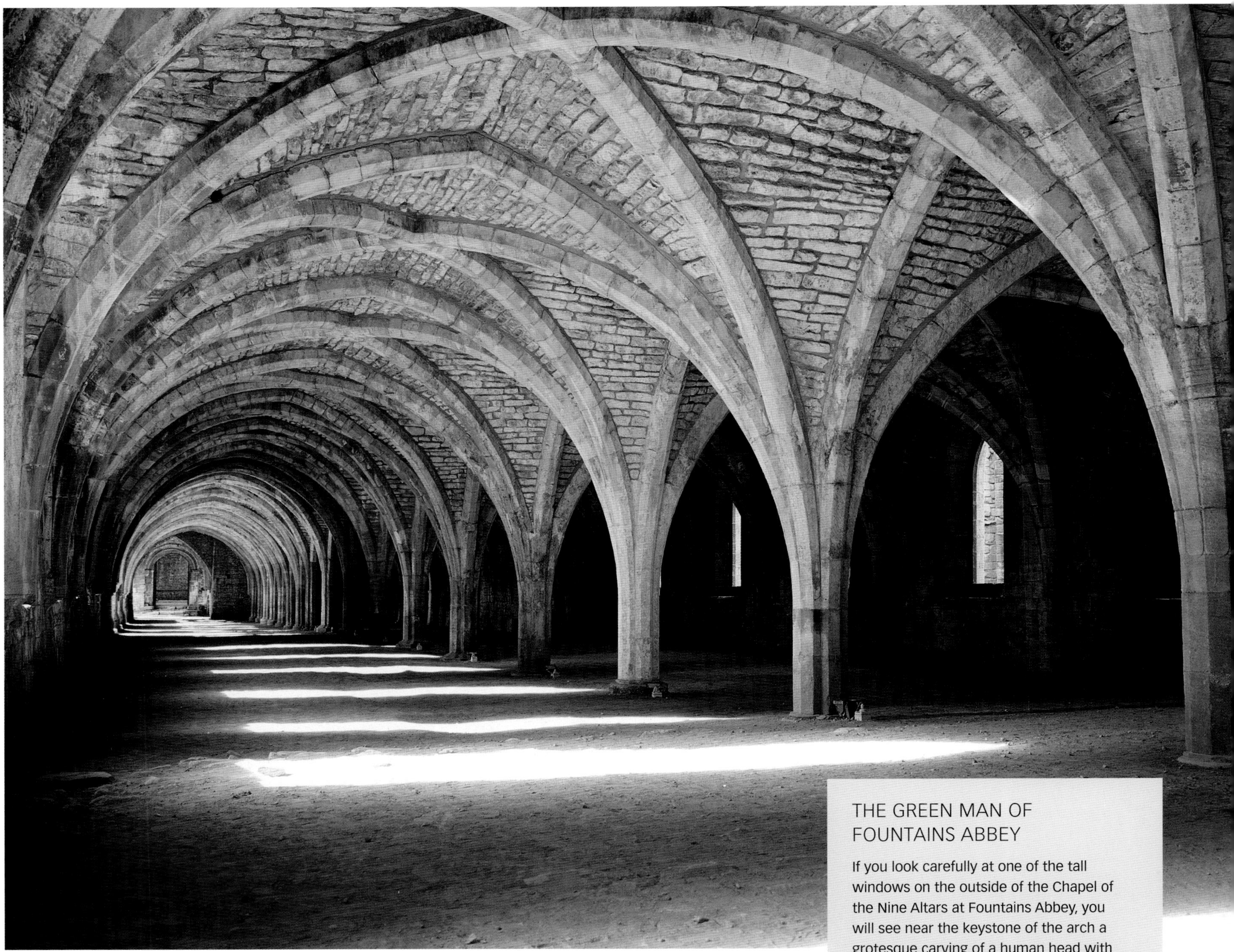

3

4

5

THE GREEN MAN OF FOUNTAINS ABBEY

If you look carefully at one of the tall windows on the outside of the Chapel of the Nine Altars at Fountains Abbey, you will see near the keystone of the arch a grotesque carving of a human head with vegetation growing out of its mouth (left).

Discovered in 1964 by Kathleen Basford, a botanist at Manchester University, this Green Man is a striking sign that the medieval builders of this magnificent Christian abbey were determined to leave a nod to the 'Old Religion'. Interestingly, an angel is carved on the corresponding keystone inside the abbey.

The Green Man is a common feature often found hidden away in the corners of medieval churches, cathedrals and other important buildings. It is a pagan fertility symbol representing the Old Religion, or the spirit of nature.

NORTH PENNINES

Five major rivers of northern England – the Tyne, Tees, Wear, Derwent and Allen – all start their lives on the high, moorland plateau of the North Pennines, a bleak, uncompromising landscape that, despite its feeling of wildness, has seen more than its fair share of industry in the past. The North Pennines – an area once aptly described as 'England's last wilderness' – lie between the Yorkshire Dales and Northumberland. The area is the highest land in the 'Backbone of England'.

The North Pennines AONB was designated in 1978 and is the second largest English AONB after the Cotswolds, covering 765 square miles (1,983sq km). It includes the Cross Fell plateau, at 2,927ft (892m) the highest point in the Pennine Chain and a milestone for walkers approaching the last section of the Pennine Way National Trail.

Topographically a high, peat- and heather-covered moorland plateau, the North Pennines drop sharply away at their western edge in the steep escarpment that frowns down over the pastoral Eden Valley in Cumbria. This formidable barrier – which creates the circumstances for the ferocious Helm Wind (see box) – was the one described by Daniel Defoe as looking like 'a wall of brass'. Oddly enough, compounds of both copper and zinc, which make up brass, were mined alongside lead, although the lead remains are more extensive, especially in Allendale and Weardale in the East Fellside area.

The geology of the North Pennines is basically typical of the Pennines as a whole: a bedrock of Carboniferous rocks in the familiar series of limestone, gritstone and shale. This is slightly tilted from the highest points in the west towards the river valleys of the Tyne and Tees to the east, where a string of reservoirs has been constructed to slake the thirst of the industrial northeast. A series of fault lines has intruded into this succession, the most important of which contains the Whin Sill, a hard igneous rock that has created some of the most spectacular landforms in the North Pennines, examples of which are the amazing High Force and Cauldron Snout waterfalls.

The Upper Teesdale section of the Pennine Way, between High Force and Cauldron Snout, is one of the most impressive on the whole 270-mile (435km) route. High Force, reached either by a concessionary path from the High Force Hotel or from the Pennine Way via the rare stunted and gin-scented juniper woods of Keedholm Scar, is not the highest waterfall in Britain but it surely must be the most impressive and powerful.

The usually peat-stained waters of the Tees plunge 70ft (21m) over a black outcrop of Whin Sill dolerite into the dismal pool

Right The Pennine Way between Widdy Bank Farm and Cauldron Snout

THE HELM WIND

The Helm Wind, which blows off the high plateau of Cross Fell into the Eden Valley, is the only wind in Britain to be given the distinction of a name.

The only British example of a föhn wind, it occurs when a northeasterly blows up and across the Pennines, tumbling over the western escarpment near Cross Fell at speeds of over 100mph (161kph) into the Eden Valley below. It can sound like an approaching express train and cause all kinds of havoc. There are tales of trees being uprooted, livestock being traumatized and even damage to buildings.

The Helm Wind is presaged by the Helm Bar, a bank of cloud that builds up over the escarpment, and is formed in the resulting vortex of wind.

1

beneath, sending up plumes of rainbow-tinted spray. Usually there are two falls dropping either side of a central buttress, which brave scramblers will try to reach, although unless the water is low and you are extremely sure-footed, it is not recommended.

Further downstream, the Tees makes a much gentler, stepped descent over columnar joints of the Whin Sill at Low Force, just above Wynch Bridge, a swinging suspension bridge that is claimed to be the first in Europe. It was originally constructed by lead miners in 1704, but the present structure was built in 1830.

The Pennine Way leads on past High Force on the western bank of the Tees before crossing it at Cronkley Farm and following the eastern bank past the dramatic rock outcrops of Cronkley Scar and Falcon Clints, to reach the next great natural water feature of the Upper Tees: Cauldron Snout.

Nothing can prepare you for your first sight of the thunderous fan of boiling water that issues from a narrow cleft in the glistening black wall of the Whin Sill. More of a cataract than a waterfall, Cauldron Snout at 600ft (180m) is the longest in England, but all that awesome power is now regulated by the dam of the massive Cow Green Reservoir above. When, in the face of much controversy, the reservoir was constructed in the 1960s, many of the traditional riverside flood meadows, including the spectacular meander known as 'the wheel of the Tees' and much of the unique arctic/alpine flora of Upper Teesdale, were inundated.

The enormous heat of the Whin Sill volcanic intrusion that created High Force and Cauldron Snout also baked the surrounding beds of limestone to create the unique crumbly 'sugar limestone' geology of Upper Teesdale. This is the reason for the internationally important flora of Upper Teesdale, which led to its designation as a National Nature Reserve (NNR) in 1963.

Dolerite crags

Another great Whin Sill highlight for Pennine Wayfarers within the North Pennines AONB is High Cup Nick, above Dufton. The classic, glaciated, U-shaped valley of High Cup Gill bites deeply into the western scarp of the Pennines, rimmed by a great horseshoe of dolerite crags at the Nick, which simply means a break in the skyline. To stand on the rim and look out west towards the fertile Eden Valley and the distant blue hills of the Lake District is a truly breathtaking experience.

Although the Ice Age relict flora of Upper Teesdale, with its rare gentians, bird's-eye primroses and Teesdale violets, is the ecological highlight of the AONB, the whole of the North Pennines is of outstanding ecological value and supports a wide range of moorland and wading birds, like the curlew and merlin. Traditional hill farming (mainly sheep) is encouraged by the designation of the Pennine Dales Environmentally Sensitive Area (ESA).

1 Peat stains the waters of the Tees at High Force **2** Mosses carpet a dry-stone wall along the Pennine Way **3** Bird's-eye primrose at Moor House National Nature Reserve **4** A curlew in Upper Teesdale

2

3

4

The North Pennines was once one of the most important centres for lead mining in the world, and the fascinating story of this now defunct industry is told at the excellent Killhope North of England Lead Mining Centre near Cowshill in Upper Weardale, where the huge iron water wheel is the centrepiece (see box). You can also visit the Allenheads and Nenthead Mines Heritage Centres, which are both close by.

The largest settlement in the area is Alston, clustered around its cobbled market square and cross. At over 1,000ft (300m) above sea level, it claims to be the highest market town in England. Set on the upper reaches of the River South Tyne, Alston has a steep cobbled main street rising to the Market Cross shelter, which was reconstructed in 1983 to replace the 1863 original that was demolished by a lorry. Many buildings in this bustling town date from the 17th century. The town also has a fine reputation for delicious, locally made specialities such as Cumberland mustard and Alston cheese.

Alston Moor grew as a lead-mining community over 400 years ago, with Alston town as the service centre for the many mining families. Alston is also the terminus for the South Tynedale railway, England's highest narrow-gauge railway.

Allendale Town, another former centre for lead mining, is still the home of the Tar Barling ceremony, which marks the end of the old year on New Year's Eve. Lighted tar barrels are carried through the town on the heads of revellers, known as 'guisers'. The ceremony appears to have originated in 1858, when high winds blew out the candles being used by the town's silver band during its annual carol service, and someone suggested using lighted tar barrels instead. Claims that this was originally a pagan festival, like the Up Helly Aa fire festival in the Shetland Islands, are now thought to be unfounded.

1 Snow-covered moorland near Ashgill Head **2** Carved sheep by Keith Alexander enhance a wall near Low Force waterfall **3** Hot-headed revellers at the New Year tar barrel procession, Allendale **4** The buildings of the Killhope water wheel and Lead Mining Centre

1

2

3

THE LEAD LEGACY

The multi-award-winning Killhope Lead Mining Centre at Cowshill (left) is the most complete lead-mining site in Britain, on the site of what, in the 1870s, was the richest lead mine in Britain.

The central feature is the 68ft (21m) diameter water wheel, built in the late 1870s to separate the lead ore from waste at Park Level Mill. The mine was started in 1853 and closed in 1910. Restoration of Killhope started in 1980, and today there is still much of the fascinating lead legacy for the visitor to see.

Equipped with hard hats and cap lamps, visitors can go down the mine to experience the working conditions of Victorian miners. On the surface, they can see how miners and their families lived, and children can dress up as 'washers' to find the precious lead ore for themselves.

4

1

2

3

4

NORTHUMBERLAND COAST

Stretching northwards from Amble-by-the-Sea to Berwick-upon-Tweed and the Scottish border, the Northumberland Coast takes in some of Britain's finest unspoiled beaches, overlooked by historic castles such as Bamburgh, Dunstanburgh and Lindisfarne.

The linear Northumberland Coast AONB covers 5 square miles (13sq km) and was designated in 1958. It includes the National Nature Reserve (NNR) of Lindisfarne and the protected seabird sanctuary of the Farne Islands.

This is a coastline that has been shaped by its history as much as by its geology and the all-powerful erosive force of the sea. The geology of the coast, however, is interesting because, at Lindisfarne and Bamburgh, the intrusive black volcanic basalt of the Whin Sill meets the sea in a series of impressive rocky headlands. The sand dunes and mud flats around Lindisfarne are important for their wildlife, particularly waders and other waterfowl, and the Farne Islands are a nationally recognized breeding ground for a large colony of grey seals.

But the Northumberland Coast is perhaps best known for the wonderful range of castles that punctuates its shore. Just inland from Amble, an attractive little town on the River Coquet, is 14th-century Warkworth Castle, owned by English Heritage. This was the birthplace of Harry Hotspur, son of the first Earl of Northumberland, and its magnificent cross-shaped keep is prominent on the skyline above the town. The impressive ruins of Dunstanburgh, also English Heritage, near the fishing village of Craster, can be reached only on foot. The fragments of John of Gaunt's huge 14th-century gatehouse stand like gigantic broken teeth overlooking the huge, wave-rounded boulders of Embleton Bay.

Bamburgh Castle, standing proud on its Whin Sill headland above the wide, sweeping sands of Bamburgh Bay, is one of England's most majestic castles and the ancient home of the kings of Northumbria. The site was first fortified in the Iron Age but the present buildings, which have often been used as the backdrop to film dramas such as *Becket* (1964), *Macbeth* (1971) and *The Devils* (1971), mainly date back to the 12th century. Bamburgh, with its pretty village green, shelters beneath the castle's massive pink sandstone walls.

But perhaps the most famous historic site on the Northumberland Coast is the island of Lindisfarne, or Holy Island, with the ruins of its pink-stoned priory (English Heritage) and

1 Lindisfarne Castle appears to grow naturally out of the crag of Whin Sill, on which it was built **2** The rocky coastline of Inner Farne **3** A puffin with a beak full of sand eels on the Farne Islands **4** Celtic cross at Lindisfarne Priory

romantic but heavily restored castle (National Trust) seemingly growing out of the Whin Sill crag on which it was originally built in the 16th century.

The present building is the result of an ambitious conversion to a private house in 1903 by the celebrated young architect Edwin (later Sir Edwin) Lutyens. The tiny rooms are full of intimately detailed design, and the windows look down on the charming walled gardens planned by Gertrude Jekyll, some well-preserved 19th-century lime kilns and a series of upturned fishing boats that are now used as sheds.

Visitors can only reach Holy Island by car at low tide, when the 1-mile (1.6km) long causeway across the mud flats and sands of the Lindisfarne Nature Reserve is exposed. Dating from the 11th century, Lindisfarne Priory was of the Benedictine order, and its monks are credited with being the originators of the famous, honey-sweetened Lindisfarne mead, which is still made on the island and is popular with tourists.

Lindisfarne was chosen by the early Christian missionaries St Aidan and St Cuthbert as their refuge from the tumult of the world. It was here in the monastery founded by Aidan that the famous illuminated manuscripts known as the Lindisfarne Gospels, now in the British Library, were written in the 7th century.

The *Anglo-Saxon Chronicle* memorably recorded the violent end of the first church on Lindisfarne following an attack by Vikings in AD 794: '… the ravages of the heathen men miserably destroyed God's church on Lindisfarne with plunder and slaughter'.

Billy Shiel's boat trips from Seahouses take the visitor to the scattered outcrops of the Farne Islands, about 1.9 miles (3km) offshore, where on Inner Farne, the largest island of the group, St Cuthbert lived in holy isolation for many years during the 7th century. The Farne Islands support a summer population of around 100,000 pairs of nesting seabirds, such as puffins and guillemots, and one of Europe's largest grey seal colonies.

Four miles (6.4km) off the Northumberland Coast, the Longstone lighthouse was built in 1825 and lived in until 1990, when it was automated by Trinity House. It was from here that Grace Darling and her father set out to rescue the survivors of a wrecked paddle steamer, the SS *Forfarshire*, when it ran aground on nearby rocks in September 1838 (see box).

The AONB supports a population of 12,500, many of whom live in the small fishing ports of Craster, Seahouses and Alnmouth. Craster is a small fishing village famous for its kippers, which are locally caught herrings prepared by families like the Robsons, using the traditional method of smoking with oakwood. Its other claim to fame is that the kerbstones of London came from its stone quarry, which closed in 1939.

AMAZING GRACE

Grace Darling, the 23-year-old daughter of William Darling, a lighthouse keeper, was looking from an upstairs window of the Longstone lighthouse in the early hours of 7 September 1838, when she spotted the wreck of the SS *Forfarshire* on the low, rocky island of Big Harcar.

William decided that the weather was too rough for the lifeboat to put out from Seahouses, so he and Grace took a rowing boat (a Northumberland coble) across to the survivors, a distance of nearly a mile (1.6km). Grace kept the coble steady in the water while her father helped four men and the lone surviving woman into the boat.

William, with three of the rescued men, then rowed the fourth man and woman back to the lighthouse. Grace remained at the lighthouse, while William and three of the already rescued crew members, who were needed on the oars, rowed back and recovered the remaining survivors.

Grace Darling, who was widely lauded for her courageous actions during her lifetime, died of tuberculosis in 1842 aged 27. She is buried with her father and mother in St Aidan's churchyard, Bamburgh, where an elaborate cenotaph close by commemorates her heroism, and a museum is dedicated to her life.

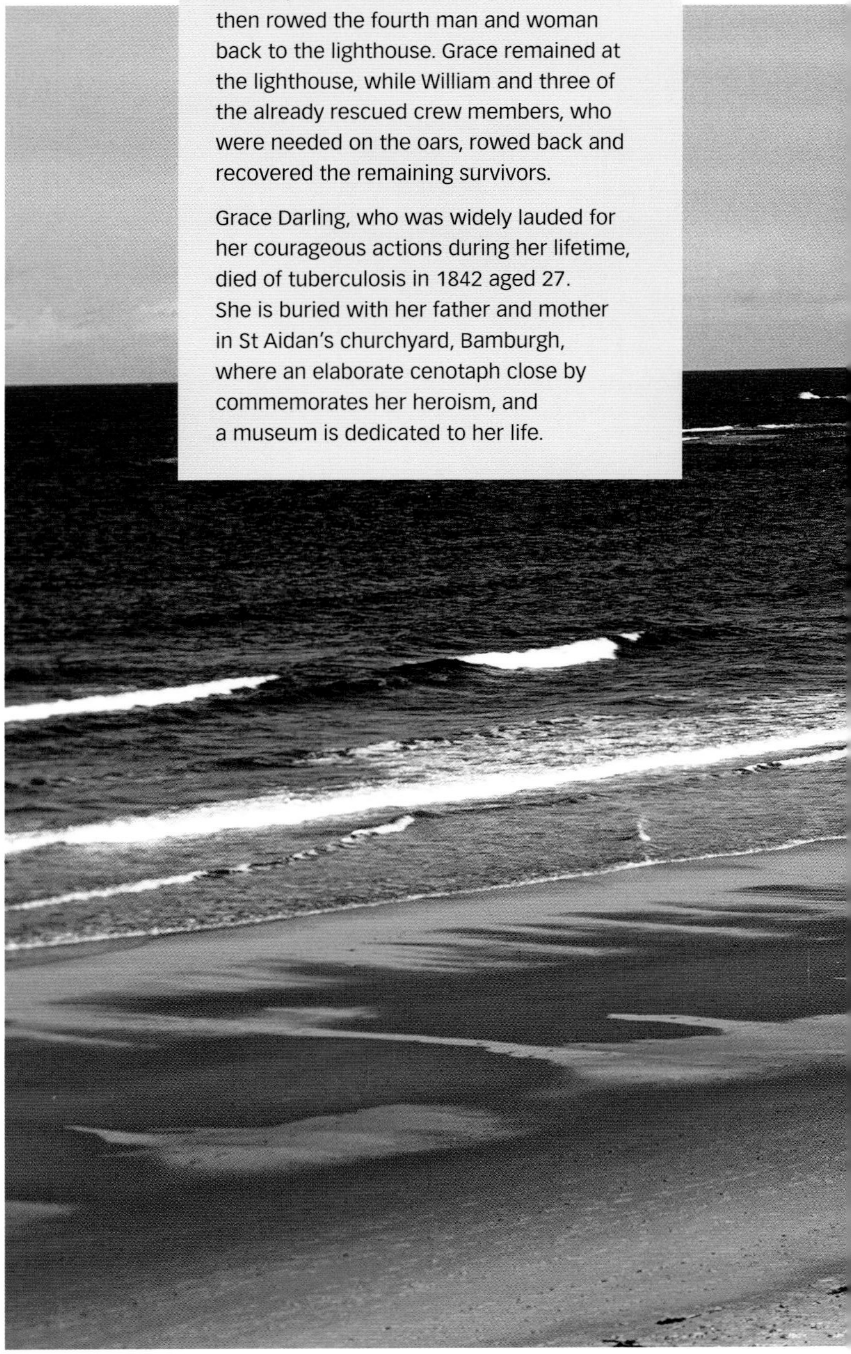

1

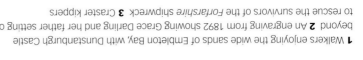

1 Walkers enjoying the wide sands of Embleton Bay, with Dunstanburgh Castle beyond **2** An engraving from 1892 showing Grace Darling and her father setting out to rescue the survivors of the *Forfarshire* shipwreck **3** Craster kippers

2

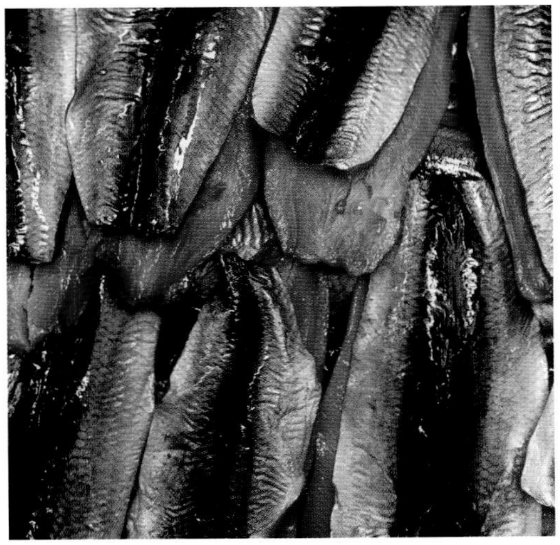

3

OTHER AONBs IN THE NORTH OF ENGLAND

The **Howardian Hills** AONB forms a distinctive undulating southern extension of the North York Moors across Ryedale and rising above the flatness of the Vale of York. It covers 79 square miles (204sq km) and was designated in 1986.

Situated on the windswept coast where Hadrian's Wall meets the Solway Firth, the **Solway Coast** AONB covers 44 square miles (115sq km). It was designated in 1964.

25
26
28
27

WALES

1

2

3

1 Lighthouse on Llanddwyn Island National Nature Reserve, Anglesey **2** Celtic cross in St Mary's church graveyard on the Gower peninsula **3** Derelict farmhouse at Clynnog Fawr, Llŷn peninsula

ANGLESEY

Some of the oldest rocks in Britain form the 125-mile (200km) coastline of the 85 square mile (220sq km) Anglesey AONB, which includes Holy Island with its busy port of Holyhead, the terminus for the Dublin ferry. It was chiefly for its spectacular and rugged coastline, which includes 31 miles (50km) of the North Anglesey, Holyhead Mountain and Aberffraw Bay Heritage Coasts, that the AONB was designated in 1966.

Geologically speaking, the ancient rocks that form the coastline are part of the Precambrian Mona Complex. Although the terrain inland is mainly a fertile plateau worn flat by the action of the sea, with low ridges and shallow valleys, the sheer limestone cliffs of the east coast and on the north coast at Holyhead Mountain – the highest point at 718ft (219m) – represent some of the most spectacular sea cliffs in Britain.

Between these are the low cliffs, coves and broad pebble beaches of the north coast, including Red Wharf Bay, Cemaes Bay and Bull Bay, and the wild sand dunes of the southwest coast at Aberffraw Bay, where the broad estuary of the Afon Cefni runs out into the Irish Sea. Just to the east of the Cefni is the Newborough Warren National Nature Reserve (NNR), one of the finest lime-rich dune systems in the country, where 560 species of plants, including the rare dune helleborine, have been identified.

On the steep northern and eastern cliffs, guillemots, choughs, cormorants and razorbills nest, while on the huge precipice of Gogarth Bay on lighthouse-topped South Stack (Ynys Lawd) on Holyhead Mountain, expert rock climbers now find their sport where local people formerly harvested gulls' eggs from the vertiginous ledges.

The distinctive, white-painted lighthouse on South Stack celebrated its bicentenary in 2009. Charles II was first petitioned as early as 1645 for a lighthouse here to warn sailors of the treacherous rocks of Holy Island. Work started on the present building, with its 92ft (28m) high tower, in 1808 to a design by Daniel Alexander. The cost was £12,000, and it was constructed from local stone quarried on Holyhead Mountain, which was transported to the island across the raging waters of the 100ft (30m) intervening chasm via ropeways and baskets.

The iron suspension bridge that eventually linked the lighthouse to the shore was constructed in 1828, replacing the precarious hemp cable bridge, which had, for 20 years, been the only way to reach the lighthouse. The light, which flashed every two minutes and could be seen for a distance of up to 10 leagues (about 30

1

2

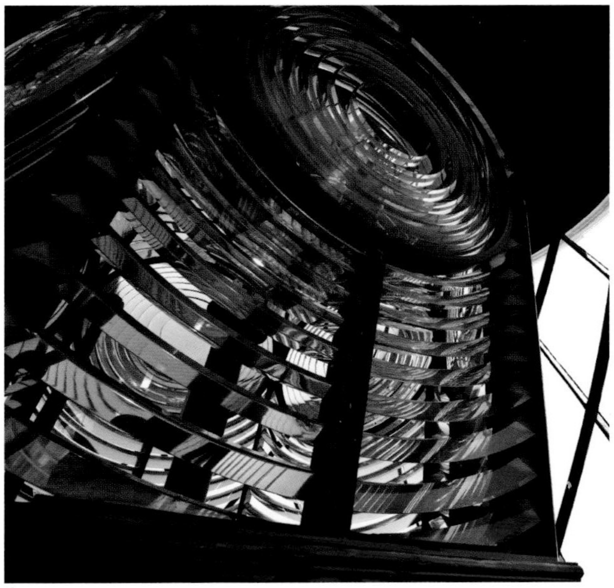
3

1 Hummocks of grass at low tide at Red Wharf Bay **2** Oystercatcher feeding on mussels along the rocky shoreline **3** The reflectors and lamp at the top of South Stack lighthouse **4** Looking down on South Stack lighthouse from the cliffs above

4

miles/50km), was fired by 21 oil lamps in the lantern room, each with its own parabolic reflector. They were eventually replaced by a diesel generator in 1938, and the lighthouse was connected to the mains electricity supply in 1963 before finally becoming automated in 1984. Astonishingly, modern optics require only a 150-watt halogen lamp for the main light.

Prehistoric remains

Anglesey was known to the Romans as Ynys Môn and was formerly the headquarters of the mysterious Celtic priesthood known as the druids. The ancient name for Anglesey, as recorded by the medieval scholar and chronicler Gerald of Wales, was *Môn Mam Cymru* (Mona, the mother of Wales).

The reign of the druids on Anglesey ended in AD 60 in a most dramatic way. Under orders from Emperor Claudius, the governor Suetonius Paulinus gathered his legionary soldiers on the banks of the Menai Strait to begin the conquest of the island. According to the *Annals* of Tacitus: 'Ranks of warriors lined the Anglesey shore, urged on by their women, shrieking like furies, dressed in burial black, while druids, with arms outstretched to heaven, cursed the invaders.' Following the invasion, Suetonius's troops cut down the 'sacred groves of the people, wherein lay their altars, red with the blood of sacrifice'.

Anglesey has a wealth of prehistoric remains. On the slopes of Holyhead Mountain, a collection of over 50 hut circles and rectangular enclosures, known as Cytiau'r Gwyddelod (Irishmen's Huts), are thought to date from the Bronze Age and were still in use in Romano-British times. The rubble-built stone rampart of the Caer y Tŵr hillfort, which encircles the mountain, dates from the late Bronze Age but was renewed and extended in the Iron Age.

Copper has been mined at Parys Mountain in the northwest of the island at least since Roman times, and probably from as early as the Bronze Age, but perhaps the most famous and most important prehistoric site on the island is Bryn Celli Ddu, translated as 'the mound in a dark grove'. Looked after by Cadw, this is a surprisingly complete Neolithic burial chamber near Newborough, whose dark confines can be entered by visitors.

Many finds indicate the wealth of Iron Age culture on Anglesey. Typical was the Llyn Cerrig Bach hoard of decorative bronze, which included a horse harness, tools and weapons, found near Valley. Most chilling, perhaps, were the two carefully crafted iron gang chains, used to secure prisoners or slaves around the neck.

Edward I's beautiful moated castle at Beaumaris was one of the last to be built in his chain of fortresses designed to quell Welsh nationalism in the late 13th century, and is a splendid example of a concentric fortress. Beaumaris – the name comes from the Norman French and means 'beautiful marsh' – is one of the largest settlements within the AONB and one of the most attractive small towns in Wales, a mixture of half-timbered houses and early Victorian terraces built by Joseph Hansom, of Hansom cab fame.

The largely 18th-century mansion and gardens of Plas Newydd (National Trust), near Llanfairpwll, is the ancestral home of the Marquess of Anglesey. The house is famous for its association with the artist Rex Whistler, and contains a large exhibition of his work.

Holyhead on Holy Island is protected by a massive, 2-mile (3km) long breakwater built when the harbour was extended in the late 19th century. Its fame rests on the fact that Thomas Telford's London to Wales turnpike – now the A5 – ended here at the embarkation point for Ireland.

1 View across the beach and sand dunes of Newborough Warren towards Snowdon **2** Bryn Celli Ddu, a Neolithic chambered barrow near Llanddaniel Fab **3** Moated 13th-century Beaumaris Castle **4** Old red post box built into a stone wall on Anglesey

1

2

3

4

CLWYDIAN RANGE

Often described as the northeastern rampart of Wales, the Clwydian Range AONB currently runs for about 20 miles (32km) south from the Dee estuary. However, as this book went to press, the Countryside Council for Wales (CCW) announced a proposed extension of the area to include the southern part of the range, as well as the Vale of Llangollen and parts of the Dee Valley. It has been suggested that the enlarged area should be called the Clwydian Range and Dee Valley AONB.

The spectacular north–south ridge of the Clwydian Range is perhaps seen at its best from the neighbouring fertile Vale of Clwyd, as a rolling open escarpment of rounded summits. The AONB, designated in 1984, currently covers 61 square miles (157sq km) of hill country between the vale to the west and the Dee estuary to the east. The proposed extension of the AONB, which is subject to consultation and confirmation by the Welsh Assembly Government, would increase the area by over 140 per cent, to 150 square miles (390sq km). Included in it would be the busy little Eisteddfod town of Llangollen; Thomas Telford's 126ft (38m) high Pontcysyllte aqueduct on the Llangollen canal (now a World Heritage Site); the romantic ruins of the early 13th-century Cistercian abbey of Valle Crucis, which is looked after by Cadw; the mountains of Ruabon, Cyrn-y-Brain, Llantysilio and Moel Fferna; and the dramatic limestone escarpment of Eglwyseg, with the ruined medieval fortress of Dinas Bran standing on a little shale hill in front.

A natural barrier of grey, 440 million-year-old Silurian rocks, the Clwydian Range has been used as a political boundary at least since the Dark Ages, when King Offa of the Mercians constructed his massive earthwork between the River Dee and the River Severn in the 8th century. The 168-mile (270km) high-level switchback is now followed by the Offa's Dyke National Trail – a popular, long-distance walking route.

The geology of the Clwydian Range is complex, with the Silurian rocks of the main ridge giving way to 350 million-year-old Carboniferous limestone in the Alyn Valley and, in the proposed extension, the Eglwyseg escarpment and Ruabon Mountains. The underlying geology gives the AONB a variety of different habitats, from the open, heather-dominated moorland of the high ridge, which rises to 1,817ft (554m) at its highest point at Moel Famau, to the small, patchwork-quilt hedged fields, woodlands and coppices of the lower slopes that extend into the vales on either side. Moel Fferna, on the southern edge of the proposed extension, stands even higher at 2,066ft (630m).

The heather moorland of the high summits is a rare and diminishing habitat, and is specially protected. This is the home of the soaring buzzard and hardy Welsh mountain sheep, which have grazed the summits to a springy turf – a delight for walkers.

The Clwydian Range is of great archaeological interest. An impressive series of Iron Age hillforts, with fine views across the vale, dominates the ridge. Foel Fenlli, a small enclosure on a 1,670ft (510m) hill, is probably the most notable. Excavations here in the 19th century produced evidence of continued occupation long after the Romans, probably by the iniquitous and tyrannical King Benlli, after whom the hill is supposedly named. Lower down in the river valleys, medieval English kings built their equally imposing castles at Rhuddlan, Denbigh and Ruthin in a vain attempt to subdue the troublesome Welsh.

At present, the Clwydian Range has no towns within its area, but many of its attractive, stone-built villages, such as Dyserth, Tafarn-y-Gelyn, Llanferres and Gelli Gynan, are now conservation areas. In the proposed extension, the town of Llangollen, famous for its international music Eisteddfod held every July, would be included. Among Llangollen's many other attractions are the Llangollen canal, built by Thomas Telford, and the black-and-white, half-timbered extravaganza of Plas Newydd, home to Lady Eleanor Butler and Sarah Ponsonby, the fabled 18th-century eccentrics known as the Ladies of Llangollen.

The area's proximity to the North Wales coastal resorts of Rhyl and Prestatyn, as well as the Dee and Wirral towns across the border in England, make it a popular day-trip destination for holidaymakers and tourists. In spite of this, it is still possible to escape the crowds on the heather-clad heights of the Clwydian Range, walking in the footsteps of King Offa.

2

1 The spectacular peaks of the Clwydian Range viewed from Bryn Alyn **2** Rhuddlan Castle and the River Clwyd

GOWER

The Gower peninsula, a lovely landscape of limestone cliffs and sandstone heaths, is the last unspoilt outpost of natural beauty in industrial South Wales, and has the distinction of being the first AONB to be designated in Britain, in December 1956.

Long favoured as a weekend destination for the industrial workers of Swansea, Port Talbot and South Wales, the fame of the Gower peninsula has now spread far beyond. Motorways such as the M4 have brought the 72 square mile (188sq km) AONB within day-trip distance of a staggering 18 million people; Bristol, for example, is only just over 80 miles (129km) away.

Its classic coastline has been recognized by the fact that the whole of it lying within the AONB – a total of 37 miles (59km) – has also been designated a Heritage Coast, entitling it to extra protection, and the area has three National Nature Reserves (NNRs), including the whole of the South Gower Coast, and many more Sites of Special Scientific Interest (SSSIs).

The topography of Gower ranges from the cockle beds of the silted-up Loughor estuary, Llanrhidian Sands and the marshes and dunes of the north coast to the superb Carboniferous limestone cliff scenery of Worm's Head, Port Eynon, Oxwich Bay and Mumbles Head on the rugged south coast, which faces the full force of the Atlantic storms.

Worm's Head, which is the rocky causeway marking the westernmost point of Gower, winds out to sea like some gigantic sea serpent and, not surprisingly, has attracted a wealth of folklore. Its name comes from the Norse *wurm*, meaning dragon, and during the right conditions, a blowhole on Worm's Head emits impressive booming and hissing noises. An old local saying is: 'The old Worm's blowing; time for a boat to be going.'

The rocky causeway is only accessible for about 2½ hours immediately before and after low tide, so you should always check the tide times before you set out on the rocky scramble to the Worm's Head. Many people, including the poet Dylan Thomas, have been stranded on the Worm.

Rhossili Bay curves in an elegant arc running north from the village of the same name, which is thought to come from *rhos* – the Welsh for moorland. The beautiful sandy beach, known locally as Llangennith Sands, is 3 miles (5km) long and backed by extensive sand dunes. Behind the beach north of the village is Rhossili Down, with its wealth of prehistoric remains.

Unrivalled microcosm

Inland, the most prominent features are the large areas of common land, dominated by long sandstone ridges covered in

Right Sunset over Worm's Head, seen from the cliffs at Rhossili

THE RED 'LAD' OF PAVILAND

The so-called Red Lady of Paviland is not quite what she seems. The virtually complete skeleton, dyed in red ochre and dating from the Upper Palaeolithic era, some 30,000 years ago, was discovered in 1823 by the antiquarian Reverend William Buckland during an archaeological dig at Goat's Hole Cave, between Port Eynon and Rhossili. It is thought to be the oldest anatomically modern human found in the UK, and the oldest-known ceremonial burial in Western Europe.

The decoration and delicacy of the bones led Buckland to believe that the remains were those of a female, possibly a prostitute or a witch, dating from Roman times. However, recent analysis has shown the skeleton to be that of a young male, while radiocarbon dating gives its age at around 33,000 years old. The Red 'Lad' is now in the Oxford University Museum of Natural History.

2

3

1

heathland and heather, and culminating in the great whaleback of Cefn Bryn, at 617ft (188m) the highest point on the peninsula and offering splendid views in all directions.

Once described as an 'unrivalled microcosm of Wales's historic wealth', there is a total of 83 Scheduled Ancient Monuments in the Gower peninsula AONB, representing most periods in history, from Upper Palaeolithic caves (see box), about 30,000 years old, through to 18th-century parkland and monuments from the Industrial Revolution.

The number of ancient burial cairns that dot the ridge of Cefn Bryn and the Neolithic Arthur's Stone burial chamber on its northern flanks show that the Gower peninsula was settled long ago in prehistory.

There are many other signs of early man's presence in the area, such as the rich collection of hut circles, cairns and burial chambers scattered across the slopes of Rhossili Down at the western end of the peninsula; the earthworks known as the Bulwark on the eastern end of Llanmadoc Hill; and the Iron Age hillfort that encircles the summit of Cilifor Top, overlooking Llanrhidian on the north coast.

Shell mounds or middens (archaeological sites made up entirely of discarded shells) that have been found along the coastline show where prehistoric man once enjoyed a plentiful supply of shellfish. The middens can still be seen on Whiteford Burrows behind Whiteford Sands.

National renown

Gower's richly varied natural environment of heath, grassland, fresh- and saltwater marsh, sand dunes and old oak woodlands makes it a haven for wildlife of national renown. Among the most important sites are the mudflats and salt marshes of the Burry inlet and Landimore marsh on the north coast, and the old oak, ash and beech woods of the deep and winding Bishopstone Valley and Bishop's Wood Local Nature Reserve (LNR) above Caswell Bay, near Newton, on the south coast.

The vast majority of Gower's population of about 10,000 people commute to nearby Swansea for work; indeed, the whole of the AONB falls within the boundary of the city. Tourism is increasingly important, as the rash of caravan sites spreading around the coast testifies. However, the older industries of farming and fishing still have their place, and the patchwork of small walled fields, stone-faced banks and hedgerows, which characterizes the interior of the peninsula, shows that the traditional small mixed farms that created the Gower landscape we see today continue to play an important part in the local economy.

4

1 Classic coastline: the deserted beach at low tide, Three Cliffs Bay **2** Ancient cave passages are a feature of the coastline of the Gower **3** The purple spikes of southern marsh orchid, a plant that thrives on the Gower peninsula **4** Collecting cockles by the River Loughor estuary – a traditional industry that has survived into the 21st century

LLŶN (LLEYN)

Sometimes described as the Land's End of Wales, the Llŷn peninsula is where the mountain heights of Snowdonia poke a rocky finger out westwards into the shimmering blue waters of the Irish Sea.

The peninsula was one of the first AONBs to be created in 1956, soon after the Gower, and it covers 62 square miles (161sq km) – roughly about a quarter – of the rocky promontory. It also includes the rugged little sacred island of Bardsey (Ynys Enlli), which surfaces like a breaching whale off the peninsula's southwestern extremity (see box).

While Llŷn may not have the mountain grandeur of neighbouring Snowdonia, it remains a stronghold of Welshness and particularly of the Welsh language, which has been spoken here for at least 1,500 years. This rich culture associated with Europe's oldest language is to be seen everywhere in the place names and the speech of the local people – for many, it is their first language.

The geology of Llŷn is closely associated with the Snowdonia massif, the marine-eroded platform that forms most of the low-lying peninsula consisting of ancient Precambrian rocks and granites. These granites reach their highest point at 1,850ft (564m) in the triple peaks of Yr Eifl, which are the stunted remains of once-great volcanoes and part of Snowdonia's famous Ring of Fire. The Welsh name of the hills means 'the Fork', and that's exactly what the three peaks resemble when seen from a distance – in English, they are also known as the Rivals.

The views from Yr Eifl – east towards the blue heights of Snowdon, south across the blue waters of Caernarfon Bay towards the Preseli Hills, and northwards towards the ancient rocks of Anglesey and the rugged promontory of Holyhead Mountain – are justly famous. Looking westward across the Irish Sea on a clear day, you may even be lucky enough to make out the outline of the Wicklow Hills, south of Dublin.

The peninsula ends in the great black cliffs of Mynydd Mawr and the headlands of Trwyn Maen Melyn, Trwyn y Gwyddel and Pen y Cil, overlooking Bardsey Sound. This spectacular coastline is the greatest glory of Llyn, and was the primary reason for its designation as an AONB. The varied geology of the peninsula is reflected in a succession of superb coastal landscapes, ranging from the steep and craggy cliffs around Aberdaron Bay and facing Caernarfon Bay on the north coast to the sandy bays, headlands and dunes of Porth Neigwl, or Hell's Mouth, on the south coast.

Inland and below the highest points, an ancient landscape of small, hedged fields and rough sheep pasture commons is linked

Right An appropriate halo of cloud settles over the 'Island of 20,000 Saints' – Bardsey Island – at the tip of the Llŷn peninsula

ISLAND OF THE SAINTS

Known as the Island of 20,000 Saints, Bardsey covers just under a square mile (2sq km) and lies about 2 miles (3km) off the Llŷn peninsula. It is reached by ferry from either Porth Meudwy or Pwllheli. The northeast of the island rises steeply from the sea to a height of 548ft (167m) at Mynydd Enlli, while the western plain is relatively flat, cultivated farmland.

The island was first inhabited in Neolithic times, and scant traces of hut circles remain. During the 5th century, the island became a refuge for persecuted Christians, and a small Celtic monastery was built. In 516, St Cadfan arrived from Brittany and, under his guidance, St Mary's Abbey was built, only to be demolished by King Henry VIII in 1537.

For centuries, the island was important as 'the holy place of burial for all the bravest and best in the land', and in medieval times, three pilgrimages to Bardsey were considered to be worth the equivalent of one to Rome.

1

2

3

4

by narrow lanes to isolated whitewashed farmhouses. Llŷn's pattern of farming remains small scale and traditional, with family farms raising sheep and cattle, and some dairying taking place where the pastures have been improved.

The Llŷn peninsula has a rich legacy of prehistory, with monuments, field systems and ancient settlements everywhere in the landscape. The most impressive prehistoric site – and surely one of the most spectacular in the whole of Britain – is the Iron Age hillfort and settlement of Tre'r Ceiri, which is situated at 1,500ft (457m) on the windy and exposed summit of the lower of the triple peaks of Yr Eifl.

Welsh-speaking

Some of the dry-stone walls, first constructed around 2,000 years ago, still stand almost to their original height, and about 150 hut circles and rectangular houses have been identified among the rocks and heather of the interior. Occupation continued here into Roman times until the 4th century AD.

Described by archaeologist Jacquetta Hawkes as 'perhaps the finest of the stone-built forts of Britain', Tre'r Ceiri, 'the town of the giants', was a stronghold of the native Ordovices. There were two large and three smaller gateways in the fine, stone-built, oval rampart, which is still 13ft (4m) high in places and features ramps leading up to an elevated walkway protected by a parapet. On the heather-covered hillside outside are further enclosures and terracing. It is believed that Tre'r Ceiri was a communal summer centre, or *shieling*, used by pastoral farmers from the lowlands beneath. But what a summer house!

The chief settlements in the AONB today are Pwllheli, the main market town for the peninsula, and the former fishing villages of Abersoch and Nefyn, which now cater mainly for an ever-increasing tourist trade. Water sports, particularly sailing small boats, diving and water-skiing, are now central to the local economy of these places. Around Abersoch, which faces east on St Tudwal's Road and into Cardigan Bay, nearly half the houses are now second homes belonging to people from the northwest of England and the Midlands.

Pwllheli has a population of nearly 4,000, with 81 per cent Welsh-speaking, so it comes as no surprise to learn that Pwllheli was where Plaid Cymru, the Welsh National Party, was founded in 1925. The town is perhaps best known today for its holiday camp at Penychain. Originally opened by Billy Butlin as part of the popular Butlins holiday camp chain in 1947, it is currently run by Haven Holidays, and has been renamed, out of respect for the Welsh language, as Hafan y Môr.

1 The three peaks of Yr Eifl, also known as the Rivals, seen from Tan y Graig beach **2** The ancient art of weaving sheep's wool on Bardsey Island **3** Iron Age hut circles at Tre'r Ceiri, believed to be a communal summer centre **4** Fishing boats moored in the estuary of the River Soch at Abersoch

30
29
33
31
32

NORTHERN IRELAND

1

2

3

1 Giant's Causeway, County Antrim **2** Mourne Mountains **3** Ballykeel portal tomb, County Armagh

1

2

ANTRIM COAST & GLENS

Backed by the lovely, deeply wooded Glens of Antrim, which run east and north to meet the Irish Sea, the coastline of County Antrim is surely among the most beautiful and geologically diverse in Britain.

The Antrim Coast and Glens was designated an AONB in 1988, and is the second largest in Northern Ireland, covering 280 square miles (725sq km). The coast is characterized by alternate sandy bays, rocky shores, high cliffs and forbidding rocky headlands, which combine to produce the dramatic scenery, while inland the beautiful wooded glens rise to meet dizzying moorland heights.

The geology of the Antrim Coast is a virtual textbook of the geology of the whole of the United Kingdom. In its astonishing variety, it is as comprehensive as anywhere in Britain, ranging from the relatively recent volcanic activity represented by the massive basalt moorland plateau to the silvery schists in the northwest, which are about 250 million years older. In between there are rich red sandstones, grey clays and completely unexpected dazzling cliffs of white chalk. This fascinating mixture is best seen at places such as Fair Head and Murlough Bay, where, in startling contrast, the chalk cliffs overlie the older red Triassic sandstones.

The Antrim coast was shaped by Ice Age glaciers and the fluctuating level of the sea, which is marked by raised beaches as seen at Southbay, near Glencloy. Other features, such as sea stacks like the White Lady, north of Garron Point, and the now high-and-dry caves in the red sandstone cliffs at Red Bay, were sculpted by the pounding action of the waves.

Among the many features of geological interest to be found along the coast are the cliffs of basalts overlying limestone from Larne to Red Bay; the great volcanic sill in the chalk of Fair Head; the similarly volcanic North Star Dyke at Ballycastle; the rich red sandstones around Cushendall; and the caves in the conglomerate rocks at Cushendun.

Seabird colonies

The shoreline is also a rich environment for marine plant, animal and bird life. Low-lying Rathlin Island, separated from the Antrim coast by Rathlin Sound, is famous for its seabird colonies. Hundreds of thousands of guillemots, razorbills and puffins breed on its low chalk cliffs and sea stacks, while fulmars soar off the cliffs near Glenarm.

With good visibility, the views from the coast extend east to the Mull of Kintyre and Ailsa Craig off the Scottish coast, while

1 Rathlin Island seen from Ballintoy **2** Waterfall in Glenariff Forest Park **3** Waterfoot beach and village at the foot of Glenariff

3

1

2

3

northwards the islands of Arran, Islay and Jura can also be seen. At the narrowest point of the North Channel at Torr Head, you are just a dozen miles from the Scottish mainland.

Fragile habitat

Inland, the plateau rises to summits including Trostan, at 1,804ft (550m) the highest point, Slieveanorra at 1,667ft (508m), and the Carncormick range at 1,437ft (438m). Rocky Slemish (1,434ft/437m) rises above the enclosed farmlands of the Braid Valley in the south.

Generally, the plateau forms a series of rugged hills, shallow valleys and internationally rare blanket peat bogs. It is an exposed and desolate area, appreciated by those seeking solitude and tranquillity. Heathers and grasses tolerant of the harsh conditions cover the hilltops, along with a uniquely specialized group of plants and animals. In some places, insectivorous plants, such as butterwort and sundew, supplement the low nutrients of the poor soil by trapping and absorbing flies, and, in the wettest boggy hollows, peat-forming sphagnum mosses dominate dark pools.

The peat, or turf, was used locally as a source of fuel, and it is still hand-cut in the traditional way in many of the glens, where the scars of peat banks are evident. However, the mechanized cutting increasingly used today is damaging this fragile habitat.

Some of these areas have been protected as National Nature Reserves (NNRs) or Forest Nature Reserves (FNRs), for example at Slieveanorra and Beaghs. But much of the upland area is still extensively grazed by sheep, and large tracts have been planted with coniferous forest, as at Slieveanorra, Breen, Glenariff, Ballycastle, Ballypatrick and Ballyboley.

Short, well-wooded glens, including the famous Glens of Antrim, dissect this high moorland plateau. The glens were formed as a result of intense glacial meltwater action at the end of the last Ice Age, perhaps 15,000 years ago. Upstream from the glens, the ice deepened pre-glacial valleys, like Glenariff and Glenballyeamon, into ice-scoured hollows filled with small loughs (lakes) and bogs.

Perhaps the most famous of the Glens of Antrim is beautiful Glenariff, where there is a well-developed forest park, a nature trail that takes in some superb waterfalls, and a visitor centre. There is another forest park at Ballypatrick in the north of the area, which includes, on the slopes of 1,322ft (403m) Crockaneel, the Neolithic Glenmakeeran court cairn tomb. The other Glens of Antrim include Glencloy, Glenballyeamon, Glenaan, Glendun and Glenshesk.

Evidence of man

The first evidence of man on the Antrim Coast is provided by the flint tools that have been found on the beaches along the coast. The Neolithic period was also marked by flint working at Ballygally and stone axe factory sites at Tievebulliagh and on Rathlin Island.

The larger stone monuments, such as Ossian's Grave in Glenaan and Glenmakeeran in Ballypatrick Forest, also date from this period, while later structures, such as raths (defended farmsteads), cashels (stone-built forts), crannogs (man-made islands) and souterrains (underground chambers), survive from early Christian times (*c.*AD 400). Medieval ruins include the friary at Bonamargy, near Ballycastle; Red Bay Castle at Cushendall; Castle Carra at Cushendun; and Bruce's Castle on Rathlin Island. The 17th-century castle at Glenarm remains the private residence of the Earls of Antrim, while Ballygally Castle is now a hotel.

The five major settlements of the Antrim Coast – Cushendall, Ballycastle, Glenarm, Cushendun and Carnlough – are conservation areas designated for their architectural interest and history.

Sometimes referred to as the Capital of the Glens, Cushendall is one of the prettiest villages on the coast, and its distinctive architecture is associated with Clough Williams-Ellis, famous for designing the Italianate village Portmeirion in North Wales. Cushendall is watched over by the medieval Curfew Tower. Famous for its Lammas fair, characterful Ballycastle is the largest of the five conservation areas, and includes many fine shop fronts along Ann Street, Castle Street and The Diamond.

1 Chalky rock face with the sea stretching out towards the distant shore at Glenarm **2** Ballycastle beach with Fair Head in the distance **3** Ossian's Grave at Glenaan **4** Colourful craft packed into Carnlough harbour **5** Edible seaweed (dulse) for sale at the Ould Lammas Fair, Ballycastle

4

5

THE LEGEND OF FINN MACCOOL

There are many legends about how the Giant's Causeway was formed, but the most persistent concerns an Antrim giant named Finn MacCool (or Fionn mac Cumhaill, in Gaelic), whose greatest rival was the Scottish giant Benandonner.

Finn decided to invite Benandonner to Ireland to challenge him in a decisive battle, so he built the causeway of huge stones across the water so that the Scottish giant could cross the sea. The other end of Finn's causeway can be seen at Fingal's Cave on Staffa, off the Isle of Mull.

Benandonner was tricked by Finn's wife, Oonagh, into thinking that Finn was a much more formidable opponent than he really was. Dressing him as a baby and placing him in a cot, she claimed that this gigantic child was Finn's baby son. Benandonner panicked and fled back to Scotland, ripping up the causeway behind him, terrified that the mighty Finn would follow.

CAUSEWAY COAST

The highlight of the beautiful Causeway Coast AONB, which extends for 19 miles (30km) from Portrush to Ballycastle, is undoubtedly the Giant's Causeway, one of the world's most celebrated geological sites.

This massive sheet of basalt cooled into the extraordinarily regular, mainly hexagonal columns of the Causeway between 58 and 55 million years ago, and is undoubtedly the showpiece of the 16 square mile (42sq km) AONB, which was designated in 1989. Three years earlier, when it was designated a World Heritage Site, the Causeway Coast had received international recognition. Now it is in the care of the National Trust.

The basalt rocks of the Causeway were formed during the Tertiary period, around 60 million years ago, as a result of violent volcanic activity. The viscous lava from nearby eruptions flowed into a depression, forming an inland lake of lava. As it cooled, it hardened, shrunk and cracked to form the approximately 40,000 columns of black basaltic rock running out into the sea towards Scotland that we see today.

Among the many spectacular features of the Giant's Causeway are the Giant's Boot, a detached, boot-shaped formation on the shore; the Giant's Organ at Port Noffer; the Giant's Harp, above Port Reostan; and the adjacent Chimney Pots, where tottering basaltic columns have become detached from the cliffs.

The bay to the north of the Giant's Causeway, known as Port na Spaniagh (the Bay of the Spanish), commemorates the wreck of the Spanish *galleass* (a large galley) *Girona*, which foundered with the loss of about 1,200 men off Lacada Point in October 1588. Captained by Don Alonso Martinez Levia, second in command of the defeated Spanish Armada, the *Girona* had taken on board the crews of two other Spanish ships, which were among 30 sunk by raging North Atlantic storms off the coast of Ireland, and they were heading north for Scotland when the tragedy occurred.

Europe's first hydroelectric tram, designed by William Traill and opened in 1883, ran between Portrush and the Causeway Hotel. It was affectionately known as 'the toast rack' because of its quaintly shaped carriages. For many people, the rattling, leisurely journey on the tram around the spectacular coast was the highlight of their holiday. The last section of the tramway finally closed in 1951.

The Giant's Causeway has had a magnetic attraction for visitors for hundreds of years, and has also drawn its fair share of folklore and legend (see box). Long before the Victorian novelist Thackeray travelled to see this 'remnant of chaos' in a small boat on a wild and stormy day in 1842, it had attracted the attention of

Left The spectacular hexagonal rocks of the Giant's Causeway

1

2

3

Samuel Johnson, the 18th-century poet, critic and writer, and his biographer, James Boswell. In his *Life of Samuel Johnson* (1791), Boswell recalled their journey made in the late summer and autumn of 1773. Boswell had asked his companion: 'Is not the Giant's Causeway worth seeing?' to which Johnson replied rather disparagingly: 'Worth seeing? Yes, but not worth going to see.'

Volcanic basalt

The oldest rocks in the AONB, found along the coast near Portrush and at the great sandy strand of White Park Bay, are sedimentary, dating from the Jurassic period (190 to 135 million years ago). The coast is also noted for its startlingly white chalk cliffs from the Cretaceous period (135 to 65 million years ago), but it is for the dark volcanic basalt that it is most famous. Features like the Giant's Causeway and the headlands of Benbane Head and Carrick-a-Rede Island, where a swinging rope bridge precariously crosses a 75ft (23m) deep and 65ft (20m) wide channel between the beetling cliffs, make this one of the most spectacular coastlines in Britain.

Fishermen originally erected a single-rope handrail bridge to Carrick-a-Rede Island over the chasm in order to check their salmon nets. This has been replaced by a two-rope handrail bridge by the present owners, the National Trust, which recommends a maximum of only eight people on the bridge at once. The reward for braving the vertiginous bridge and reaching the island is witnessing a wonderful range of seabirds, and experiencing a glorious, uninterrupted view across to Rathlin Island and on towards Scotland.

The clifftops and ledges of the Causeway Coast provide a rich habitat for a variety of plants, such as the sea aster, sea pink and white sea campion, while the cliffs are home to seabirds such as the razorbill, guillemot and puffin, the peregrine falcon, the raven and the rare coastal member of the crow family, the chough.

Human settlement on the Causeway Coast is confined to the small harbours and inlets and a few farmsteads further inland. On the headlands above, the ruined strongholds of Dunluce Castle, between Portrush and Bushmills, and Kinbane Castle, northwest of Ballycastle, watch over the coast. Dunluce, once home of local landowners the MacQuillans and, later, the MacDonnells, dates from the 14th century, and Kinbane, reached by a steep path and across slippery rocks, was another MacDonnell stronghold, dating from the 16th century.

The major settlement on the Causeway Coast is Bushmills, home of the famous Bushmills whiskey distillery, which is claimed to be the oldest in the world. Bushmills lies at the heart of a lush barley-growing area and has the other vital ingredients necessary for the successful distilling of whiskey: abundant clear water and plentiful supplies of peat.

1 Giant's Boot, an oddity found near the Giant's Causeway **2** The harbour at Portrush **3** Brightly painted whiskey barrels decorate the old distillery at Bushmills **4** Giant's Head, with Dunluce Castle in the background

4

MOURNE MOUNTAINS

The rugged granite peaks of County Down's Mourne Mountains are celebrated in Percy French's famous song (see box, overleaf) all over the world, and they form the core of the 220 square mile (570sq km) AONB, which was designated in 1986.

The Mourne Mountains AONB is one of the largest and most important in Northern Ireland, and has for many years been considered the prime candidate for the province's first, long-awaited national park. It contains all the peaks of the compact Mourne range, including Slieve Donard, which, at 2,789ft (850m), is the highest point in Northern Ireland.

The Mournes are formed of a hard, grey granite, and are among the youngest mountain ranges in the UK. They were created only 50 million years ago, a mere blink of the eye in geological terms, when a vast block of shale subsided deep within the earth's crust, forcing up the molten granite. Subsequent weathering and the sculpting action of Ice Age glaciers completed the majestic picture. The power of the glaciers is vividly seen at Hare's Gap – a classic mountain pass shaped by the passage of ice – between Slievenaglogh and Slieve Bearnagh.

But the AONB boundary takes in much more than the Mournes, with their sharply eroded peaks, tors and jagged rock pinnacles. To the north, the isolated outlying mountain mass of Slieve Croob (1,752ft/534m) and Legananny Mountain (1,407ft/429m) are separated from the main range by the forested Castlewellan Valley, while to the south, around Kilkeel, Rostrevor and Warrenpoint, the land drops away through moorland, woodland, field and farm towards Carlingford Lough.

Mourne granite

The wildlife of the Mournes is dominated by the acidic moorland slopes of the hills, where the heather supports populations of red grouse and their predators, such as the peregrine falcon and buzzard. Three species of heather – cross-leaved heath, bell heather and ling – are found in the Mournes, and other acid-loving plants include bog cotton, roseroot, harebell, marsh St John's wort, wild thyme and heath spotted orchid.

You are most likely to meet sheep grazing high in the mountains, and the birdlife includes the raven, wren, meadow pipit, grey wagtail, stonechat and snipe. The stately golden eagle, a distinguished former inhabitant, was last seen in the Mournes in 1836.

Dark swathes of commercial coniferous forestry fringe the hills at places like Tollymore, Rostrevor, Castlewellan and Donard Park. Only one small pocket of extensive native sessile oak woodland survives as the Rostrevor Forest Nature Reserve (FNR) on the mountain slopes behind Rostrevor.

Mourne granite has been in demand for building stone since the 18th century, and the many quarries in the hills are said to have paved industrial Lancashire, a short journey across the Irish Sea, during the Industrial Revolution. Later, the stone was used to construct reservoirs, like the Silent Valley Reservoir, built between

1 The Ben Crom Reservoir from the Brandy Pad path through the Mournes **2** Silent Valley Reservoir provides drinking water for the city of Belfast

2

1923 and 1933 to dam the Kilkeel River and provide drinking water for the city of Belfast. Silent Valley was formerly known as Happy Valley but, since being flooded by the reservoir, it is devoid of birdlife and is therefore now silent.

The granite was also used in the construction of the amazing 3ft (1m) wide, 5–6ft (1.5–1.8m) high, 22-mile (35km) long Mourne Wall, which encloses the 14 square mile (36sq km) catchment area of the reservoir, and goes up hill and down dale with scant regard to the steep contours.

The Mourne Wall crosses no fewer than 15 of the Mourne summits, and was constructed between 1904 and 1922 to define the boundaries of the area of land purchased by the Belfast Water Commissioners in the late 1800s. This followed a number of Acts of Parliament allowing the establishment of a water supply from the Mournes to the growing industrial city of Belfast.

Following a fundraising drive in 1993, the National Trust purchased nearly 2 square miles (5.2sq km) of land in the Mourne Mountains. This included part of the highest peak of Slieve Donard and nearby Slieve Commedagh, the next highest peak in the range at 2,516ft (767m).

Evocative names

Many of the Mourne Mountains have names beginning with that distinctive word 'slieve', which comes from the Irish *sliabh* and simply means mountain. Examples are Slieve Donard, Slieve Commedagh, Slieve Lamagan and Slieve Muck. There are also a number of evocatively named features among these hills, such as Pigeon Rock, Buzzard's Roost, the Cock and Hen, the Devil's Coach Road, the Brandy Pad, and the curiously named Pollaphuca, which means 'hole of the fairies or sprites'.

The Brandy Pad, which winds its way from the head of the Annalong Valley to Hare's Gap before dropping down to the Trassey River, gets its name from the pedlars and smugglers of wines, spirits and tobacco who used the track during the 19th century. It is now a popular walking route through the Mournes, offering a good path and fine views.

Today, the Mourne Mountains are a playground for tourists, hillwalkers, mountain bikers and rock climbers. A countryside centre covering the Mournes AONB is located in the neat little seaside town of Newcastle, the main settlement on Dundrum Bay. Named after a now-demolished castle built in the late 16th century at the mouth of the Shimna River, Newcastle has recently benefited from a multi-million pound refurbishment. The smart restored promenade has won a number of national awards, including a Civic Trust Award for Excellence.

1

THE MOUNTAINS OF MOURNE

The song *The Mountains of Mourne* is normally sung to the traditional Irish tune Carraig Donn (or Carrigdhoun), and is typical of many of songwriter Percy French's works about the great Irish diaspora of the 19th century. Contrasting the artificial attractions of the city with the natural beauty of the singer's homeland, the song is considered a little too whimsical for traditional folk audiences today.

French, who was born in 1854 in County Roscommon, wrote his first successful song in 1877 while he was studying to become a civil engineer at Trinity College, Dublin. He is now best known for his comic songs, such as *Phil the Fluter's Ball, Slattery's Mounted Foot* and *Are Ye Right There Michael?* – a song ridiculing the state of the rail system in rural County Clare.

Having enjoyed a long and successful career as one of Ireland's best-known songwriters and entertainers, French died in Formby, Lancashire, in 1920.

1 The pass of Hare's Gap and the Mourne Wall **2** Depiction of poet Percy French on Newcastle promenade, where 'the Mountains of Mourne sweep down to the sea' **3** Gorse growing on the Mournes **4** Horse-riding on Tyrella beach, with the Mourne Mountains in the background

2

3

4

RING OF GULLION

The Ring of Gullion AONB in South Armagh protects the most complete and spectacular example in Britain of what geologists call a ring dyke intrusion, and includes the beautiful area of farmland, woodland, bog and heathland that surrounds it.

The 59 square mile (153sq km) Ring of Gullion AONB includes the whole of the mountain ring and, to the west, the Dorsey Enclosure and the valley of the Cully Water and the Umeracam River, which separate the hills from the rolling ice-sculpted landscape towards Crossmaglen and Cullyhanna. In the northwest, the ring dyke runs through the higher ground of the Fews, where it is marked by sharp rocky hills with distinctive heathland vegetation. This provides very little grazing, which is how the Fews came by its name. The eastern boundary is the Newry Canal and the Newry River, flowing towards Carlingford Lough beneath the Anglesey and Flagstaff Mountains.

Debate has raged for years on exactly how the ring of volcanic intrusions, known as dykes, formed around the central peak of Slieve Gullion, which, at 1,880ft (573m), provides a magnificent viewpoint of this geological wonder of Britain. At one time, it was thought that the ring was a caldera – the vast collapsed crater of a volcano into which lava was extruded in layers. But now it is thought that the lava was intruded deep underground, to be unearthed by later weathering and erosion. Whatever the cause, this tremendously powerful volcanic interlude is thought to have happened in relatively recent geological times, in the Tertiary period of perhaps 65 million years ago.

The surrounding rocks are much older, dating from the Silurian period of 400 million years ago, and also include intrusions of granite, which took place 390 million years ago. The whole of this tortured landscape has been shaped and modified by the passage of ice, and many of the upstanding outcrops show signs of the grinding power of Ice Age glaciers.

The harder volcanic rocks of the Ring of Gullion resisted the erosive powers of the glaciers, while fault lines, such as that now filled by the lake of Camlough, were scoured out by moving ice and flowing meltwaters. The peaks of mountains such as Slieve Gullion stood aloof from the ice, and the areas that had been breached by the glaciers later became migratory routes through which people, animals and plants moved into the area.

As well as eroding parts of the landscape, the moving glaciers also deposited silts and clays, creating small rounded hills known as drumlins, shaped by the retreating ice as conditions warmed and the last Ice Age ended 15,000 to 12,000 years ago. This drumlin landscape stretches from the west coast into South Armagh.

Left The Ring of Gullion, one of the geological wonders of Britain

1

2

3

The glaciers left behind a rich habitat of semi-natural woodlands, such as the Hawthorn Hill Forest Nature Reserve, which includes oak, beech, rowan and Scots pine. These support populations of red squirrel and, in winter, provide shelter for Slieve Gullion's famous herd of wild goats.

Only small fragments of the Ring's once-extensive lowland bogs still exist, but the craggy hills of Slieve Gullion and some of the surrounding peaks are still clothed by large areas of heather moorland. Cross-leaved heath and bog asphodel thrive in the wetter areas, while the drier moors support ling, bell heather and western gorse. The only major lake in the area is Camlough, meaning 'crooked lake'. A glacially formed 'ribbon' lake, it supports populations of mute swan, great crested grebe, moorhen and reed warblers in the reed beds.

Myths & legends

The Ring of Gullion has the reputation of being Ireland's mystery mountain range, arising from its association with many myths and legends. Chief among these is the legend of the Cattle Raid of Cooley, in which the fabled hero Cúchulainn is reputed to have defended Ulster single-handed against the army of Queen Maeve of Connaught (see box).

More solid evidence of past occupation is provided by the wealth of prehistoric remains in the area, notably the 20 large stone-built tombs dating from the Neolithic period, perhaps 6,000 years ago. These include the Ballymacdermot and King's Ring court tombs, which are two of the best examples of their kind in Northern Ireland. The monument at Ballykeel is an outstanding example of a portal tomb, while the South Cairn on the summit of Slieve Gullion is the highest passage tomb in Britain.

Top among the places to visit in the Ring of Gullion area is Derrymore House at Bessbrook. Two miles (3km) from Newry and in a picturesque estate, this elegant 18th-century thatched cottage is where the Act of Union, uniting Great Britain and Ireland to form one country, was drafted before its signature in 1800. The house is now a National Trust property.

Also worth visits are the Áras an Chairdinéil ó Fiaich Heritage Centre in Slatequarry Road, Cullyhanna, where you can listen to songs and poems from South Armagh, and the Slieve Gullion Forest Park, which covers 4 square miles (10sq km) near Newry and offers spectacular views of the surrounding countryside. It is also the starting point for a 6-mile (10km) scenic drive.

The waymarked 36-mile (58km) Ring of Gullion Way runs through the Ring of Gullion AONB from Newry to Derrymore House at Bessbrook, mainly on forestry tracks and open hillsides, but there are also significant road sections. There are wonderful views extending to Carlingford Lough and the Mourne Mountains.

1 Great crested grebe **2** Cairn on top of Slieve Gullion **3** The *Brown Bull of Cooley* by local artist Michael McKeown, on the Ballymascanlon roundabout **4** Looking from the Ring of Gullion towards the Newry River and Carlingford Lough

2

3

Mediterranean feel

Mount Stewart House is famous for having one of the finest and most unusual gardens in Europe. The mild climate of Strangford Lough allowed extraordinary levels of planting experimentation, and the gardens at Mount Stewart reflect the design skills and planting artistry of Edith, Lady Londonderry, in the years following 1915. The formal gardens, which include the Shamrock Garden, the Sunken Garden, the Spanish Garden and the Italian Garden, have a strong Mediterranean feel about them, while the wooded areas support a wide range of plants from all over the world.

Mount Stewart has been in the hands of the Stewart family (later Vane-Tempest-Stewart) since 1744, when Alexander Stewart (1699–1781) bought the estate, then known as Mount Pleasant, apparently with money acquired through sales of linen. His son, Robert Stewart, became the 1st Marquess of Londonderry and, after his death in 1821, the house was left to his son, also Robert, better known as Viscount Castlereagh, a prominent Tory politician.

The next owner of the house was his half-brother, Charles, 3rd Marquess of Londonderry (1778–1854), who married the heiress Lady Frances-Anne Vane-Tempest and spent £150,000, a considerable sum of money at the time, on the refurbishment and enlargement of the newly named Mount Stewart. Charles was also largely responsible for the elegant, 11-bay and porticoed Georgian house we see today.

Other visitor attractions include the Scrabo and Delamont Country Parks, which have splendid walks overlooking the lough; the Exploris Centre, one of Europe's largest aquaria and seal sanctuaries, at Portaferry; the Strangford Lough Wildlife Centre at Castle Ward; and the Quoile Countryside Centre. There is also a newly opened Wildfowl & Wetlands Trust centre at Castle Espie.

OTHER AONBs IN NORTHERN IRELAND

A playground for nearby Belfast, the **Lagan Valley** AONB covers 8 square miles (21sq km) and is centred on the Lagan Valley Regional Park and the winding River Lagan. It was designated in 1965. The **Lecale Coast** AONB was designated two years later and covers 12 square miles (31sq km) of the extensive sand dunes between Strangford Lough and the Mournes, and is famous for its seal colonies.

The **North Derry** AONB was designated in 1966 and covers 500 square miles (1,295sq km) of sandy strands backed by the imposing 984ft (300m) peak of Binevenagh, which is now, sadly, partly cloaked in conifers. Designated in 1968, the **Sperrin Mountains** AONB is 3,900 square miles (10,000sq km) of sparsely populated moorland penetrated by narrow glens and deep valleys. It rises to the 2,224ft (678m) high Sawel Mountain.

1 Boats moored in Strangford Lough **2** Garden sculpture of Lady Londonderry as a child in the grounds at Mount Stewart House **3** A reconstructed crannog (man-made island) at the Castle Espie Wildfowl & Wetlands Trust centre on Strangford Lough

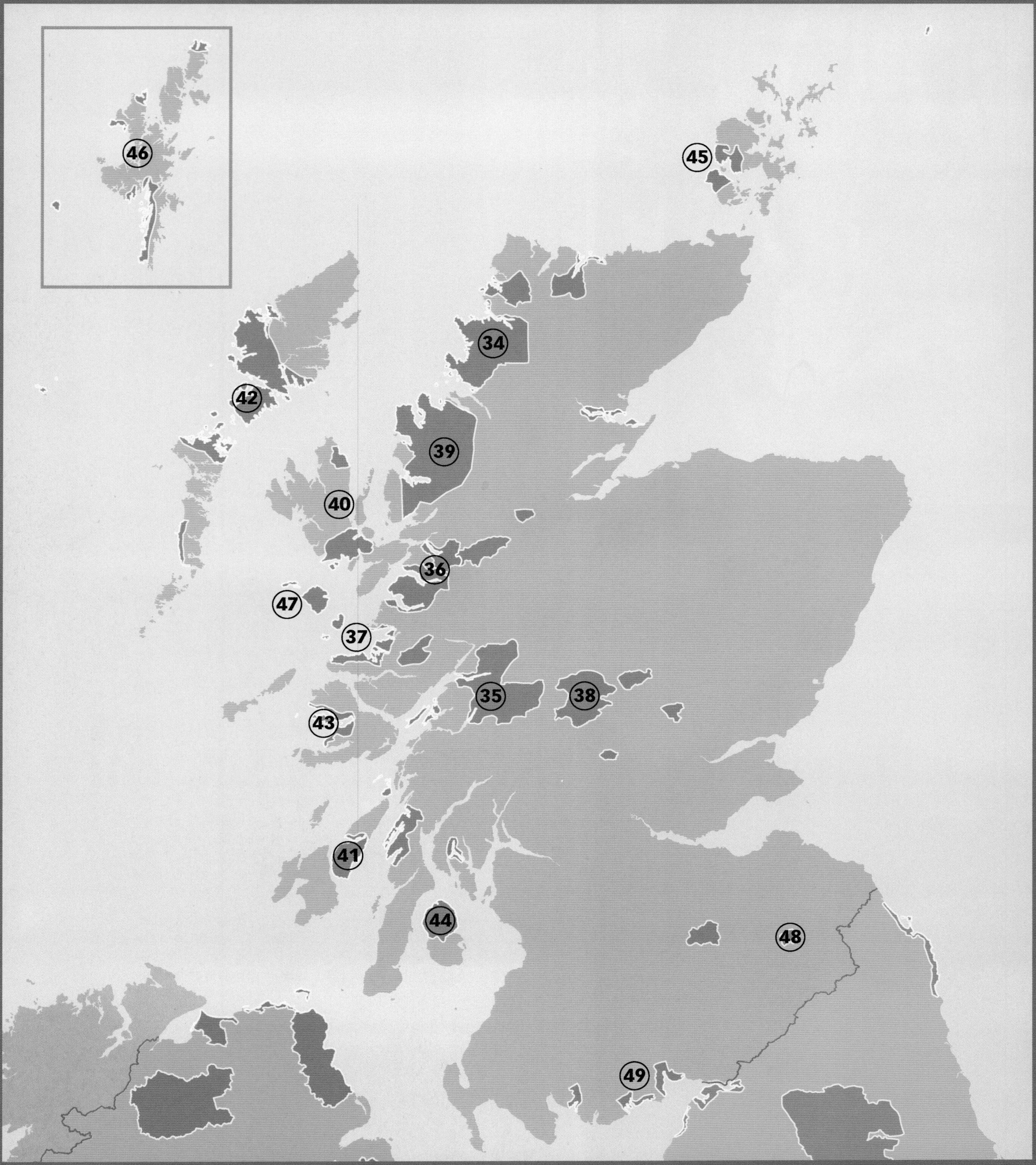
46
45
34
42
39
40
36
47
37
35
38
43
41
44
48
49

SCOTLAND

Highlands

Islands

Southern Uplands

1

2

3

1 A climber surveys a sea of clouds from the summit of Ciste Dhubh in the Kintail NSA **2** A winter view of the Neolithic stone circle of the Ring of Brodgar, Orkney **3** Colourful seashells on a Rum beach

ASSYNT-COIGACH

Suilven, Stac Pollaidh and Quinag represent some of the most spectacular mountains in Britain, and they form the rugged heart of the 348 square mile (902sq km) Assynt-Coigach National Scenic Area (NSA).

This wild and rocky NSA stretches from Eddrachillis Bay in the north to the two-pronged Loch Broom in the south, on the remote northwest coast of Scotland. Described by the respected mountaineer W H Murray as 'a mountain landscape unique in the whole Scottish scene', the area is distinguished by 'loch and cnocan' (small lakes and hills) scenery on a plain of incredibly ancient, ice-worn gneiss (metamorphic rock). This hillocky bedrock contains chains of serpentine lochs and necklaces of hundreds of smaller, jewel-like lochans, punctuated by the dramatic sandstone-cored mountains.

In *Highland Landscape*, his 1962 survey for the National Trust for Scotland, Murray vividly described the scene: 'More than a hundred… lochs and lochans lie around. When the sky is bright they scintillate, brilliantly blue, and all about them wild hills rise stark. When the sky is heavy, and grey mists twist among the mountain spires, they glint whitely or lie black and fathomless.'

The strange shapes of the towering peaks, which rise so abruptly from this lochan-studded base, are the remains of much younger sandstones that have been sculpted over aeons by wind, frost, ice and rain. And the sugar-loaf shape of Suilven, at 2,398ft (731m), is the strangest and most impressive of them all.

Strange monster

The conical summit is perhaps seen to best effect from the tiny fishing village of Lochinver at the head of Loch Inver, where it peeps over the horizon like some approaching behemoth. Murray claimed it was Sutherland's most famous mountain. Seen from the west coast or from the east, near the head of Strath Oykel, it rears its isolated head like a strange monster rising out of the sea.

It has a long summit ridge with three separate tops: the spire-like Meall Bheag ('Little Hill', 2,001ft/610m) and Meall Mheadhonach ('Middle Hill', 2,372ft/723m) at the eastern end, and at the western end, the rounded tower of Caisteal Liath ('Grey Castle', 2,365ft/721m), all surrounded by beetling cliffs.

Naturalist Frank Fraser Darling was impressed by Suilven. 'There is only one Suilven and it is undoubtedly one of the most fantastic hills in Scotland. It rises 2,309ft out of a rough sea of gneiss… probably the Dolomites would be the nearest place where such an extraordinary shape of hill could be seen.'

Left Morning light on Stac Pollaidh in the foreground, with Suilven beyond

1

2

3

Other peaks in the NSA, which contains some of the wildest and most rugged scenery in Scotland, include Ben More Coigach at 2,438ft (743m), Ben More Assynt at 3,274ft (998m), Cul Mor at 2,785ft (849m) and Quinag at 2,654ft (809m). Reached by a restored pathway leading from the car park at its foot is Stac Pollaidh – often anglicized to Stack Polly – one of the most popular peaks for walkers. Its bristling, shattered sandstone crest rises to 2,008ft (612m) above Loch Lurgain.

Stac Pollaidh was also eloquently described by Murray in *Highland Landscape*: 'Stac Pollaidh is a sandstone mountain. Seen from the west it soars up sharply conical. It has in fact a long summit ridge running west to east, shattered into pinnacles. The mountain seems to bristle like a porcupine.'

With its vast bulk, Ben More Assynt dominates the Inchnadamph Forest on the eastern boundary of the NSA. It is quite different from the other peaks because, unlike them, it rises to the east of the Moine Thrust, an earth movement that took place 400 million years ago and which shaped so much of this part of the Highlands.

Western light

The deeply indented coastline of the region is no less dramatic than the interior. Eddrachillis Bay has a scattering of islands, which catch the constantly changing western light, while the long narrow sea loch of Loch a' Chairn Bhain and its tributaries of Loch Glendhu and Loch Glencoul are surrounded by towering peaks and bare, rugged hills. In the south, off Achiltibuie, the delightfully named Summer Isles – the largest of which are Tanera Beg and Tanera Mor – form a broken seaboard in sharp contrast to the solid mass of Ben More Coigach to the east.

Lochinver, with its sandy coves to the north, is one of the most beautiful and popular resorts on the wild, rocky coast of Assynt. Still an important fishing village, it also caters for anglers and hillwalkers, and is the base for boat trips to the many islands that dot Enard Bay, including Soyea Island (Sheep Island).

In recent years, two important National Nature Reserves (NNRs) at Inverpolly and Inchnadamph have been de-designated and effectively wiped from the map, after their landowners refused to renew their agreements with Scottish Natural Heritage (SNH). The owners of the 41-year-old Inverpolly NNR, which is used extensively for deer stalking, said they could not reach an agreement with SNH, and the NNR was officially de-designated in 2003. Conservationists claimed that such nationally important sites should not rely on the whim of landowners, and SNH itself said it had taken the decision 'with considerable disquiet'.

The same fate befell the Inchnadamph NNR, which has the most extensive limestone habitats and vegetation in northwest Scotland, after its owners claimed the commitment to manage the land for nature conservation did not fit in with their commercial objectives, which included retaining a deer herd for a sporting programme of culling. While expressing its disappointment, SNH pointed out that the site remains nationally and internationally important for both its habitats and geology, and that public access rights remain unchanged.

There is still much to see at Inchnadamph, which is part of the North West Highlands Geopark. It includes the famous Bone Caves of Creag nan Uamh, in the glen of Allt nan Uamh, 2 miles (3km) south of the village of Inchnadamph. The caves, which are a Site of Special Scientific Interest (SSSI) and a Scheduled Ancient Monument, give a unique glimpse back in time. Human remains dating back at least 4,500 years have been found here, along with animal bones going back 45,000 years, such as polar bear, lynx, hyena and hippopotamus, all now obviously extinct in Scotland.

One NNR remains in the NSA, at Loch a' Mhuilinn on the northeastern shore of Eddrachillis Bay, 2.5 miles (4km) south of Scourie. The best time to visit Loch a' Mhuilinn is in the spring, when a carpet of wildflowers covers the woodland floor, and the trees drip in a fairytale coating of lichen and moss.

1 Quinag viewed through an open field gate on the Stoer peninsula **2** Highland lochan near Suilven **3** Achmelvich Bay **4** The Bone Caves of Creag nan Uamh in the former Inchnadamph NNR **5** Female pine marten in the undergrowth at Ardnamurchan peninsula

4

5

BEN NEVIS & GLENCOE

This 392 square mile (1,016sq km) National Scenic Area (NSA) contains two of Scotland's greatest and best-known scenic gems: the melodramatic valley of Glencoe and the highest mountain in Britain, Ben Nevis, which stands at 4,406ft (1,343m).

From Glen Spean in the north to Glen Kinglass in the south, the NSA covers the western extremity of the Grampian Mountains. The eastern boundary is marked by the remote outpost of Rannoch train station on the West Highland Line on bleak Rannoch Moor; the western by the mouth of Loch Leven beyond Ballachulish.

The diverse scenery of the NSA is characterized by the intricacy of its geology. Granite dominates the Ben Nevis, Glen Etive and Rannoch Moor areas, while Glencoe is mainly of volcanic origin. This complicated geology has created landforms that vary from smooth and grass-covered hills to jagged and precipitous crags, like the northern face of Ben Nevis, which provides some of the hardest rock-, snow- and ice-climbing routes in Britain. Lower down, there are wide areas of peaty moorland studded with lochans (small lochs), such as the great moor of Rannoch, and swift-running streams that have carved well-wooded glens, such as Glen Nevis and the fjord-like Loch Leven and Loch Etive.

1 Red deer stag in Glen Etive **2** Two of the Three Sisters of Glencoe – Beinn Fhada (left) and Gearr Aonach (centre) – as seen from the glen

1

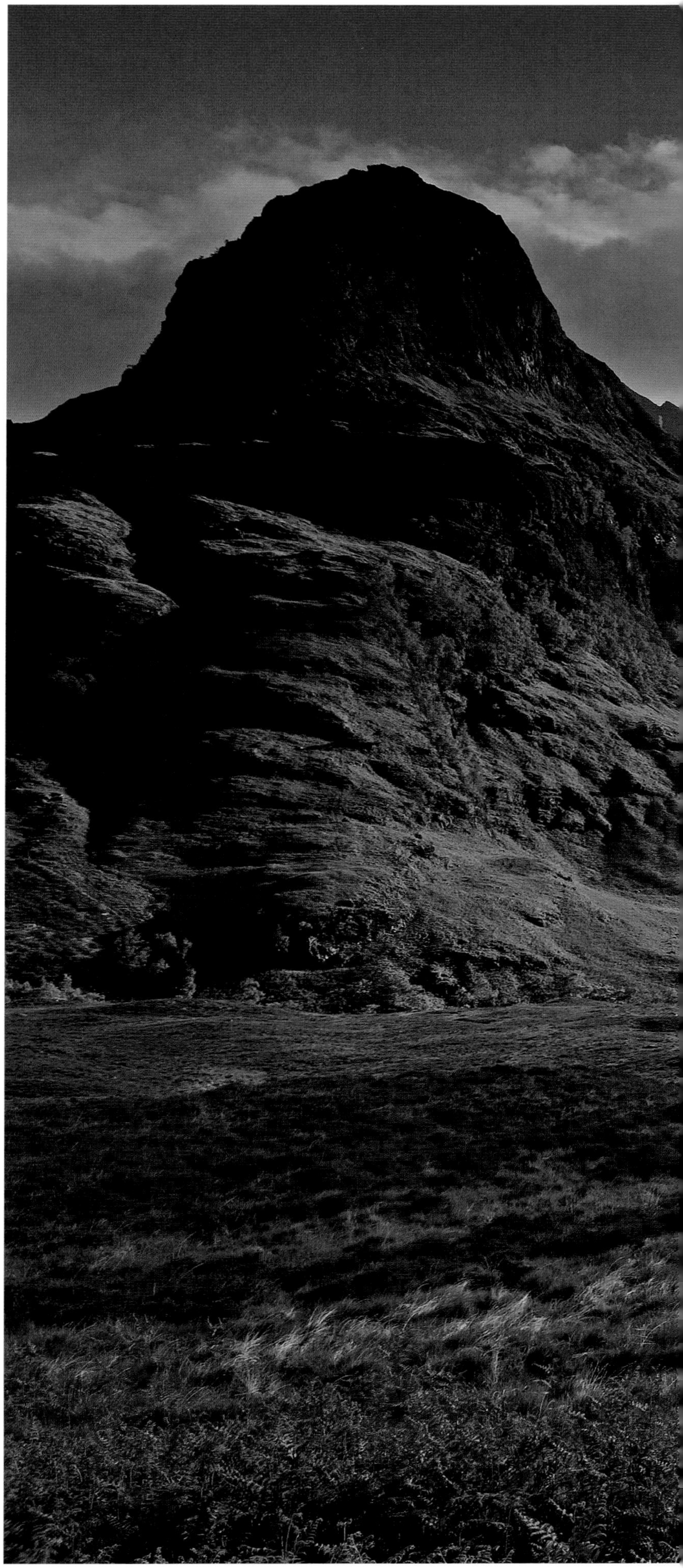
2

TWENTY YEARS ON THE BEN

The Ben Nevis Observatory on the summit of the mountain was built in 1883 by the Scottish Meteorological Society. A team of three meteorologists lived for weeks on end in the tiny building, making regular observations of the rainfall, temperature, wind speed and sunlight for 20 years until the observatory closed, despite storms of protest, in 1904.

Observations made between 1884 and 1901 recorded an average mean temperature of 31.4ºF (that is, half a degree below freezing, or –0.33ºC); an annual average of 756 hours of sunshine (an average of about two hours a day); an average of 157.7in (4,005mm) of rainfall; and an average barometric pressure of 25.3in of mercury (857 millibars). In winter, wind speeds exceeded 150 miles per hour (241kph).

The maximum depth of snow of 141in (nearly 12ft, or 3.6m) was recorded in April 1883. Photographs from *Twenty Years on Ben Nevis* by part-time meteorologist William T Kilgour, published in 1905, show the observatory covered in fantastic confections of ice and snow.

Ben Nevis

No other part of Britain has greater relative relief than Glen Nevis, which runs south then east from the former Georgian garrison town of Fort William (which is excluded from the NSA), under the massive southern shoulder of Ben Nevis. Many people have compared the wooded middle section of the gorge created by the Water of Nevis to a Himalayan valley. From the pastoral lower reaches, the glen climbs through glorious oak, alder, pine and birch woodlands on a narrow path above the boiling waters.

The upper glen is a place of peaceful, almost alpine, meadows, enhanced by the backdrop of the tremendous 350ft (106m) leap of the Steall waterfall as it crashes down the lower cliffs of Sgurr a' Mhaim. To reach the waterfall, you have to cross a vertiginous, three-stranded wire bridge over the rushing Water of Nevis. The glen is walled to the south by the smooth-sided ridge of the Mamore Range, which includes 14 peaks above 3,000ft (914m). South of that is the fjord-like trench of Loch Leven, with the former aluminium plant industrial village of Kinlochleven at its head. Kinlochleven was one of the first towns in Britain to have street lighting via hydroelectric power from the Blackwater Dam.

The northern side of Ben Nevis is dominated by Coire Leis. Described by the distinguished mountaineer W H Murray as 'the most splendid of all Scottish corries', Coire Leis is flanked by Carn Mor Dearg, Aonach Beag and the tremendous northern buttresses of Ben Nevis. Here stands the CIC hut, a refuge for generations of climbers on 'the Ben', built in 1929 as a memorial to mountaineer Charles Inglis Clark who died during World War I. It is now maintained by the Scottish Mountaineering Council.

The usual 'tourist' route to the summit of Ben Nevis is known as the Pony Track, and was constructed in 1883 in order to get building materials to the summit for the observatory (see box). It ascends gradually from the Glen Nevis Visitor Centre near Achintee up to the broad saddle that contains Lochan Meall an t-Suidhe (the Halfway Lochan). A steep and fairly arduous series of zigzags then takes you up the broad west face of the Ben, where you eventually reach the relatively flat summit and the remains of the observatory. The route involves 4,400ft (1,340m) of ascent and is a serious undertaking that usually lasts between three and four hours.

Glencoe

Beyond Loch Leven is the dramatic valley of Glencoe, lying between the ultimate scramblers' challenge of the Aonach Eagach and the truncated spurs known as the Three Sisters. These run down from Bidean nam Bian, at 3,743ft (1,141m) the highest mountain in Argyll, like the clenched knuckles of a fist.

The Victorians, with their taste for the melodramatic, dubbed Glencoe 'the Glen of Weeping'. Charles Dickens hated the place,

2

3

4

1 Ben Nevis viewed from Inverscaddle Bay in Ardgour **2** The Steall waterfall beneath the Mamores **3** A skier enjoys the snow in the Ben Nevis range **4** A party of British Boy Scouts climb Ben Nevis, Britain's highest peak, in 1938

and claimed its very recollection made him shudder. Glencoe was, he wrote, 'perfectly terrible', and 'an awful place... there are scores of glens, high up, which form such haunts as you might imagine yourself wandering in, in the very height and madness of a fever'. The travel writer H V Morton waxed even more hysterical in his *In Search of Scotland* (1929). 'Here is a landscape without mercy,' he wrote. 'As far as Glencoe is concerned, the first germ of life has never struggled from the warm slime.'

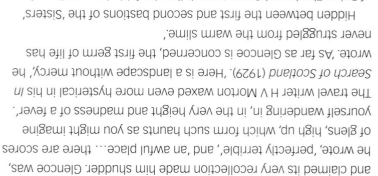

Hidden between the first and second bastions of the 'Sisters' of Beinn Fhada and Gearr Aonach lies the fabled Lost Valley of Glencoe, Coire Gabhail (pronounced 'Corry Gale'). Traditionally, Coire Gabhail was where the MacDonalds hid the cattle they had stolen from their neighbours in the days when cattle rustling was something of a croft industry in the Highlands. Certainly, the broad green sanctuary of Coire Gabhail is well hidden from the old road, which passes through the glen far below.

At a height of about 1,200ft (365m), the flat, green meadow floor of Coire Gabhail is enclosed by the precipitous walls of Gearr Aonach and Beinn Fhada, which sweep round to the great buttresses at the head of the valley and the pass of Bealach Dearg, eventually leading up to the unseen summit of Bidean nam Bian. If you are lucky, you'll be greeted by the magnificent sight of a golden eagle soaring effortlessly on fingered wings above the bealach.

Forever associated with the massacre of the MacDonalds in 1692 (see box), Glencoe is now owned and managed by the National Trust for Scotland. Neighbouring Glen Etive does not have the same awe-inspiring grandeur of Glencoe, and it is guarded at its northern end by the imposing twin sentinels of Buachaille Etive Mor and Ben Starav and threaded by the beautiful River Etive. To the east are the barren, lochan-strewn expanses of the National Nature Reserve (NNR) of Rannoch Moor. Ringed by the great mountains of Black Mount, it is perhaps the most desolate and godforsaken scene in the whole of Scotland.

Murray played down the bleakness of Rannoch Moor in his *Highland Landscape* survey of 1962. 'It has in itself outstanding beauty, derived in part from its many lochs and islands, its tufted surface and heather, and from the great array of fine mountains encircling it, from Schichallion to Buachaille Etive Mor. This unique setting makes it an integral part of the mountain scene. Neither could be what it is, nor appear so distinguished, without the other.'

The perfect mountain cone of Buachaille Etive Mor (the Great Herdsman of Etive), which stands sentinel at the entrance to Glencoe as the A82 motorist completes the 10-mile (16km) traverse of the flat wastes of Rannoch Moor, reminded Murray of a Gothic cathedral or a Neolithic arrowhead. In his classic *Mountaineering in Scotland*, published in 1947, he described the Buachaille 'the most splendid of earthly mountains'.

1

2

1 Whitewashed crofts in Glencoe village **2** Black Mount viewed from Rannoch Moor **3** A golden eagle carries food back to its eyrie **4** An oil painting of *The Massacre of Glencoe* by James Hamilton (1853–94)

THE MASSACRE OF GLENCOE

A sign above reception in the 18th-century Clachaig Inn at the foot of Glencoe reads: 'No hawkers or Campbells.' The memory of the apparent treachery of the Campbells, who rose up and slaughtered their hosts the MacDonalds in Glencoe, is obviously still fresh in the memory, although today, of course, the message is left more for the amusement of tourists than in any sense of lasting revenge.

It was in early February 1692, under orders from John Dalrymple, Secretary of State for Scotland and Lord Advocate, that Captain Robert Campbell and about 120 members of his regiment were billeted with the MacDonalds in Glencoe, where they were received with traditional Highland hospitality. The reason behind the order and the subsequent massacre was that Dalrymple was incensed that Alastair Maclain, the MacDonald clan chief, had been late in pledging his allegiance to William and Mary, the new monarchs, and wanted to teach the clan a lesson.

The massacre began simultaneously in three settlements – Invercoe, Inverrigan and Achnacon – although the killing took place all over the glen as the fleeing MacDonalds were pursued. A total of 38 members of the clan were slaughtered, and a further 40 women and children died of exposure after fleeing into the hills when their homes were burned down.

3

4

KINTAIL, GLEN AFFRIC & KNOYDART

Kintail

The 60 square mile (155sq km) Kintail National Scenic Area (NSA) adjoins the Glen Affric NSA and covers the mountainous head of Loch Duich, including the famous ridge of the Five Sisters of Kintail and the Saddle across Glen Shiel.

The Scottish mountaineering writer W H Murray considered that Kintail contained the essence of the West Highlands. 'In Kintail,' he wrote in *Highland Landscape* (1962), 'nothing lacks; all things culminate. It is the epitome of the West Highland scene.' The great glory of the Kintail NSA is the splendid hills that crowd together around the head of Loch Duich on either side of Glen Shiel. In fact, three mountain ranges terminate here: Beinn Fhada (the Long Mountain) at 3,386ft (1,032m); the Five Sisters of Kintail (culminating in Sgurr Fhuaran) at 3,504ft (1,068m); and the South Cluanie Ridge, which extends for 9 miles (14km) and includes seven Munros (Scottish mountains over 3,000ft/914m, see box, page 184) leading up to Aonach air Chrith (3,350ft/1,021m) and the Saddle (3,314ft/1,010m), reached via the formidable Forcan Ridge.

Much of the northern side of Glen Shiel, including the Five Sisters ridge and remote Beinn Fhada between Glen Lichd and Glen Choinneachan, is now in the safe hands of the National Trust for Scotland (NTS). Its Kintail estate extends north to the difficult-to-reach but spectacular Falls of Glomach, one of the highest waterfalls in Britain and a Site of Special Scientific Interest (SSSI), where the Glomach Burn tumbles 367ft (112m) contained within

1

the walls of a narrow ravine. There is an NTS visitor centre at Morvich at the end of the eastern arm of Loch Duich. The glens radiating from Loch Duich are uniformly steep-sided and narrow, with rushing burns that cascade through waterfalls and pools lined with birch, rowan and alder, to eventually reach the sea loch.

Where the loch turns west to meet Loch Alsh, the junction is guarded by the romantic and much-photographed castle of Eilean Donan, a heavily restored structure on an ancient island site, now linked to the mainland by a causeway. The castle, which incorporates a memorial to the Clan Macrae, was bombarded by a British frigate during the Jacobite Rebellion in 1719. Shortly after, a Jacobite force, which included a contingent from Spain, was defeated at the Battle of Glen Shiel near the mountain still known as Sgurr nan Spainteach (Peak of the Spaniards).

1 The breathtaking beauty of the Five Sisters of Kintail **2** The Dog Falls amid the rugged scenery of Glen Affric

2

1

Glen Affric

Glen Affric is flanked on the north side by some of the highest mountains of the Northwest Highlands, shapely conical peaks rising to Carn Eige at 3,881ft (1,183m) and Mam Sodhail at 3,875ft (1,181m). These are all ranged above a long, glaciated valley, with steep sides and a broad floor, threaded by the River Affric.

In the valley lie the two great lochs of Loch Affric and Loch Beinn a' Mheadhoin. The lower slopes of the hills are clothed in one of the most beautiful remnants of the ancient native Caledonian pine forest, with a leavening of birches and a sufficiently open canopy to permit the growth of purple-hued heather and blaeberry.

No wonder the glen is often claimed to be Scotland's loveliest. From the rich woodland in the east to the stark mountains of the upper glen, where all is moor and heather, it displays a fine variety of scenery. Fiona Leney, writing in the unpublished 'Landscape of Scotland' report, commissioned by the Countryside Commission for Scotland in 1974, perhaps best caught the essence of the glen: '… the area maintains a sense of wilderness, less rugged than the remote area of North West Scotland and has a grandeur and classic beauty that is not found in the bleaker lands to the north.'

Surrounded by mature pines, Affric Lodge at the eastern end of Loch Affric was built in Victorian baronial style in 1864 as a hunting lodge for the 1st Lord Tweedmouth. It enjoys the same use today.

2

3

4

Knoydart

Adjoining the Kintail NSA at Glen Sheil Forest, and northwest of the busy ferry port of Mallaig, the Rough Bounds of Knoydart are one of the remotest and most sparsely inhabited parts of Britain. The Knoydart peninsula between Loch Nevis and Loch Hourn contains some of the wildest scenery in Scotland, protected in this 153 square mile (395sq km) NSA. Thomas Pennant, the Welsh naturalist, writing about Loch Hourn in 1772, claimed: 'There is no part of our dominions so remote.'

No roads cross this uninhabited wilderness and, as W H Murray noted: 'Travel within the Knoydart peninsula goes on foot.' He added that the numerous glens and tracks, free from traffic, offer excellent walking through wild country, but warned that venturing away from the tracks was 'extraordinarily rough'.

The Sound of Sleat coastline contributes much to the beauty of the NSA, and the archetypal western sea lochs of Nevis and Hourn both have wide outer stretches that give way to narrow, fjord-like inner lochs as they penetrate deep into the mountains.

The winding sea loch of Loch Hourn in the north ends in sandy Barrisdale Bay, where it bites into an intensely glaciated mountain mass. Here, to the south, 3,343ft (1,019m) high Ladhar Bheinn, pronounced 'Larven', the most westerly Munro in mainland Scotland, and Beinn Sgritheall, 3,196ft (974m) high, to the north, are the reigning summits. Both these hills are serious expeditions for experienced hillwalkers only, due to not just their height but also their remoteness.

Loch Nevis in the south presents a sunnier, more open aspect, thanks to the lower hills that flank its southern side. The bays of Loch Nevis, such as Inverie and Sandaig, add further interest, while the narrow upper reaches are dominated by soaring peaks, such as Sgurr na Ciche at 3,412ft (1,040m), whose rocky spire has been compared with the Matterhorn, and Garbh Chioch Mhor at 3,323ft (1,013m).

The deep, finger-like glens of Knoydart, such as Gleann na Guiserein and Gleann an Dubh Lochain, have long, stepped profiles, where broad marshy flats and lochans alternate with steep, wooded gorges. Most of the mountain slopes consist entirely of rocky scree and crags, while the lower slopes are enriched by bracken, sedges and rough grasses. Remnants of former oak, ash and birch woodlands still survive in the rocky ravines, where the burns rush down to meet the main glens.

The Kintail and Knoydart NSAs are among the best places in Scotland to see the magnificent golden eagle – the king of the Highland skies – soaring on its massive 6.5ft (2m) wings above the glens and lochs. Although many people mistake the common buzzard for an eagle – they are sometimes known as the 'tourists' eagle' – once you have seen the real thing, you'll never forget it.

1 The ancient native woodlands of Glen Affric **2** A mature Scots pine (known as a 'granny') rising out of its bed of heather **3** Eilean Donan Castle, Loch Duich **4** Foxgloves growing beside Loch Hourn

MORAR, MOIDART & ARDNAMURCHAN

Essentially a coastal area, the Morar, Moidart and Ardnamurchan National Scenic Area (NSA) covers 52 square miles (135sq km) and extends south from the Morar peninsula to the rocky northern shores of Ardnamurchan. It is centred on Loch nan Uamh and Loch Moidart, and the broad reaches of the Sound of Arisaig.

Four main areas make up this NSA, all of which offer fine seaward views of the distant and amusingly named cocktail of Hebridean Small Isles: Rum, Eigg and Muck (see pages 208–211). When seen from the western shores of Ardnamurchan, the impressive plug of volcanic pitchstone known as An Sgurr (1,289ft/393m) on Eigg is especially prominent.

The heavily indented rocky coastline of remote northern Ardnamurchan has successive bays reaching east from Sanna Bay past Port Ban to the enclosed sandy reaches of Kentra Bay. Small former fishing villages, such as Portuairk, Sanna, Fascadale, Kilmory and Ockle, punctuate the shoreline, backed by bare rocky hills such as Meall nan Con at 1,434ft (437m) and Beinn Bhreac at 1,171ft (357m). The rocks of Ardnamurchan are of volcanic origin, and headlands like Rubha Carrach, Ockle Point and Rubha Aird Druimnich impart a stern ruggedness to the scene.

Across the flat moss and sands of Kentra, steep woodlands enclose the slopes of Loch Moidart inland to Ardmolich, while the islands of Eilean Shona and Eilean Tioram partly block its mouth. Loch Moidart has a sheltered, enclosed aspect, with rounded, wooded islands punctuating the braided channels of the loch, and the villages of Ardtoe, Newton of Ardtoe, Kentra and Shielfoot shelter in its bays.

Coastal castles

The picturesque ruins of Castle Tioram stand on the rocky tidal island of Eilean Tioram, where the River Shiel enters Loch Moidart. It is one of a remarkable group of coastal castles in Argyll and the Isles, and is closely linked to the long history of seafaring in the Western Highlands. The castle was once an important centre and significant in Gaelic culture.

Constructed during the 13th to 14th centuries, when the surrounding area was considerably more populated than it is today,

Left An aerial view of Castle Tioram on Loch Moidart

the castle ceased to be the family residence of the Clanranalds in the early 20th century, when they built a more comfortable house in South Uist, and it subsequently fell into disrepair. But as a romantic ruin, standing at the heart of the loch and mountain landscape, it still presents an iconic image of Highland Scotland. The Scottish author J M Barrie (1860–1937) took a story associated with Castle Tioram of a maid who was tied to a rock on the beach for stealing silver and used it in his popular children's 'fairy play' *Peter Pan*, first published in 1901.

Commando country

Compared with Loch Moidart, Loch Ailort and Loch nan Uamh are more open in aspect, with heather- and scrub-covered islets and a richly wooded shore of rocky promontories leading out into the Sound of Arisaig. The NSA takes in the loch-crowned peninsula of Ardnish in South Morar, and follows the railway towards Arisaig on Loch nan Ceall and out to the promontory of Rubh' Arisaig beyond Arisaig House. This grey stone mansion, originally built in 1864 and much altered in the 1930s, is now a luxurious but homely guest house, with additional self-catering properties set within landscaped gardens and woodland.

Gleann Máma and Glen Beasdale lead out beneath the hills of Beinn nan Cabar and Sidhean Mór to the coast near Druimindarroch, before the A830 sweeps round to Arisaig and, eventually, to the port of Mallaig. From here, it is a 30-minute journey by ferry to Armadale on the Isle of Skye. Following the opening of the Skye Bridge on the A87 across the Kyle of Lochalsh in 1995, the Mallaig–Armadale crossing is the only way the visitor can now follow Bonnie Prince Charlie's route 'over the sea to Skye' by 'bonnie boat'.

There are strong associations with Bonnie Prince Charlie (Prince Charles Edward Stuart) and the 1745 Rising (see box) in the area. Loch nan Uamh (the Loch of the Caves) is traditionally supposed to have witnessed both his arrival from Eriskay in July 1745 and his departure 14 months later. He set up his headquarters in nearby Borrodale, and Castle Tioram on Loch Moidart was where the rebels' guns, swords and pistols were stored. A simple cairn erected by the 1745 Association in 1956 on the shores of Loch nan Uamh marks the traditional point from where he finally set sail for France in September 1746, after the disaster of Culloden.

The area around the loch is also known as commando country – it was used extensively for some of the toughest commando training during World War II, which has left its own legacy on the landscape. Cul Doirlinn, Inverailort and Kentra were among the villages used to garrison the troops.

1

2

3

1 Colourful ropes front a crofter's cottage in the remote village of Ockle **2** A proud fisherman with his boat at Arisaig **3** This plaque on Loch nan Uamh marks the spot where Bonnie Prince Charlie embarked for France in 1746 **4** View to the Isle of Eigg from Sanna Bay

THE PRINCE IN THE HEATHER

Attempts to restore the Stuart dynasty to the British throne ended in the failed Jacobite Rebellion of 1745, and the defeat of Bonnie Prince Charlie at Culloden in the following year.

After the Culloden disaster, when 5,000 of Charles's ill-equipped troops were massacred by the Duke of Cumberland's well-drilled army of 9,000 redcoats, Charles (the French-speaking grandson of James VII of Scotland) went on the run through the Highlands for 20 weeks. With a price of £50,000 on his head, a massive sum at the time, he slept rough in caves in the hills and, aided by loyal Highlanders, walked for hundreds of miles through the heather. This included a spell on the Isle of Skye sheltered by Flora MacDonald, which became the stuff of legend.

Charles eventually fled back to France from Borrodale on Loch nan Uamh aboard the French frigate *L'Heureux* in 1746. He ended his days a disillusioned alcoholic in Rome in 1788.

LOCH RANNOCH & GLEN LYON

Loch Rannoch

The 187 square mile (484sq km) Loch Rannoch National Scenic Area (NSA) includes Loch Rannoch, the Black Wood of Rannoch, Glen Lyon and the summit of Ben Lawers, in the mountainous heart of the ancient kingdom of Breadalbane.

Loch Rannoch is an open, spacious loch, running east to west from the Bridge of Gaur to Kinloch Rannoch, famous for the varied and beautiful woodlands that surround it. Pine, birch, oak, ash, larch, cypress and juniper trees abound, while the southern slopes are taken up by the great Black Wood of Rannoch, one of the best surviving examples of Scotland's once-extensive native Caledonian pine forest.

The eastern end of the loch runs into Loch Dunalastair, a reservoir created by a hydroelectric dam. But with its shoreline of reed and willow beds, it nevertheless presents a pleasing contrast with the larger Loch Rannoch.

North of Loch Dunalastair, shapely Schiehallion (3,553ft/1,083m) appears from most viewpoints as an almost perfect cone, rising in splendid isolation, but it is actually a long, whaleback ridge running west to east (see box). West from Schiehallion, the peaks of Carn Mairg, Carn Gorm and Meall a' Mhuic separate Rannoch from beautiful Glen Lyon.

Ben Lawers, at 3,983ft (1,214m) the highest mountain in the region, is famous for its arctic/alpine flora, making it a Mecca for botanists. Among the rare survivors from the last Ice Age found on its exposed flanks are purple saxifrage, alpine gentian, alpine lady's mantle and alpine cinquefoil. This unique flora was seriously threatened by over-grazing under ancient tenancy agreements, but Ben Lawers is now in the hands of the National Trust for Scotland (NTS), and its future seems secure. However, the NTS was guilty of erecting a somewhat incongruous, circular visitor centre on the southern slopes of the mountain above Killin, which continues to attract much criticism.

The reason for the very special assemblage of arctic/alpine flora on Ben Lawers is its peculiar geology. The Ben Lawers–Caenlochan schist is part of the Dalradian group of shales, laid down about 650 million years ago, later compressed and metamorphosed during the Caledonian period some 150 million years later. These originally limey shales were transformed into calcareous, mineral-rich mica schists, ideal for the unique type of flora found on the mountain. Thus this rich collection of plants, normally found only in the high

1

2

1 Sunset over Loch Tummel, with Schiehallion on the left **2** Trig point on top of Ben Lawers **3** The deadly spikes of the insectivorous common sundew **4** Mathematician Charles Hutton assisted Charles Mason in the Schiehallion Experiment

THE SCHIEHALLION EXPERIMENT

Schiehallion's isolated position and regular shape led English astronomer Charles Mason (1728–1786) to select it in 1774 for a ground-breaking experiment to try to establish the weight of the Earth. The deflection of a pendulum caused by the gravitational pull of the mountain provided an estimate of the mean density of the Earth, from which its mass and a value for Newton's gravitational constant could be deduced.

Mason, in fact, turned down the commission to carry out the work and it was eventually coordinated by Nevil Maskelyne, Astronomer Royal. He was assisted in the task by the mathematician Charles Hutton (1737–1823, left), who devised a graphical system to represent large volumes of surveyed heights. These later became known as the familiar contour lines found on Ordnance Survey maps.

Charles Mason's other claim to fame was that he was responsible, with Jeremiah Dixon, for surveying the celebrated Mason–Dixon line between the American states of Pennsylvania and Maryland.

3

4

1

Arctic or in the European Alps, is due to a series of coincidences – a small stratum of ideal rock on a mountain that is so high that the habitat has existed unchanged since the departure of the Ice Age glaciers 10,000 years ago.

Glen Lyon

Glen Lyon is separated from Loch Rannoch by the broad summit of Carn Mairg. Said to be the longest glen in Scotland, it exhibits an enormous diversity of scenery along its 25-mile (40km) length.

Deeply entrenched between Carn Mairg and mighty Ben Lawers, the glen gradually descends from these wild, bare mountains around Cashlie, where the remains of five ancient Celtic forts have been discovered, towards Fortingall. Beyond Allt Conait, it becomes a broad strath (valley) traversed by the leisurely loops of the River Lyon. On the northern bank, the white-walled Meggernie Castle is majestically set in the midst of woodlands and approached by a famous long avenue of lime trees.

Meggernie Castle was the traditional home of the Campbells of Glen Lyon, built by 'Mad' Colin Campbell in 1593. Other lairds have included Captain Robert Campbell, the man who led the government troops at the massacre of the MacDonalds in Glencoe in 1692 (see page 165). It is also reputed to be haunted, most stories deriving from the time of its occupation by the Menzies of Culdares. A Menzies laird is said to have murdered his beautiful young wife in a fit of rage and cut her body into two in order to conceal the crime. Guests at the castle claim to have seen the upper part of a woman's body floating through the air and, during restoration work at the castle in the mid-19th century, workmen are said to have unearthed the skeletal remains of her torso.

In Glen Lyon, the woodlands clothing the lower slopes of the mountains contrast well with the barer but colourful higher slopes, and as you descend the glen, the farmlands of the strath and the woodlands of the lower slopes become ever richer and more varied. At each turn of the road, a new scene of river, wood, mountain and meadow is revealed until, at the Pass of Glen Lyon, the river rushes through a tight, rocky gorge, closely screened by magnificent canopies of beech, to open finally on the pleasant meadows of Fortingall.

The Scottish mountaineer W H Murray wrote in his *Highland Landscape* survey of 1962: 'Glen Lyon has no counterpart in Scotland. Other glens, like Affric or Tilt, show a similar change from desolate upper reaches to lower fertility, as may be seen too in the Cairngorms. Others, like Glen Nevis, possess some unique feature of gorge, or loch, or waterfall, or forest, not to be seen in Glen Lyon. But there is none that displays such varied loveliness of river and woodland scene and maintains it unmarred throughout so great a length of changing landscape.'

1 A venerable Scots pine and remnants of the ancient Caledonian forest at Glen Lyon **2** Golden-hued birch woodland **3** Autumnal colours above a waterfall and an old stone bridge in Glen Lyon

2

3

WESTER ROSS

This 561 square mile (1,453sq km) National Scenic Area (NSA) is the largest of them all, and includes six of the greatest mountain groups in Scotland, including the spectacular Torridon peaks of Liathach, An Teallach, Slioch and Beinn Eighe.

Often described as the last great wilderness of Scotland, Wester Ross is the embodiment of Highland grandeur. Add to that the superb coastline in the northwest, including Gruinard Bay, peaceful Loch Ewe, Loch Torridon and Loch Gairloch, and you have the personification of the Western Highlands. It therefore comes as no surprise that Wester Ross has been proposed as one of Scotland's possible national parks.

The area is of particular interest to geologists because many of these amazing mountains consist of red Torridon sandstone, and some, like layered Liathach, are topped with startling white quartzite summits, which are often mistaken by tourists for snow. The great Scottish mountaineering writer W H Murray described Liathach as 'the most soaring mountain in the north', and seen in the classic view reflected in tranquil Loch Clair, it certainly assumes a majesty far beyond its modest 3,458ft (1,054m).

But Liathach is only one of a whole series of magnificent mountains that rise imperiously from the Applecross, Letterewe, Torridon and Fisherfield forests, which are generally treeless and 'forests' only in the ancient hunting sense. Murray described the fierce, jagged outline of An Teallach at 3,484ft (1,062m) as 'one of the half dozen most splendid mountains in Scotland', and its eastern cone of Toll an Lochan as 'one of the greatest sights in Scotland'. Few who have explored the rugged splendour of that mountain fastness would disagree.

Beinn Eighe (3,314ft/1,010m) has the distinction of being the first National Nature Reserve (NNR) to be designated in Britain, in 1951, and it is famed for its arctic/alpine flora and fauna. The mountain shares that distinctive quartzite cap with Liathach, and is by far the largest of the Torridon peaks.

Highland grandeur

The ancient Caledonian pinewoods that cloak its lower slopes are one of the Beinn Eighe NNR's greatest assets, and they are home to rare creatures such as the wildcat and pine marten, and birds including the Scottish crossbill and redstart. But it is the fact that the reserve stretches from sea level to more than 3,280ft (1,000m) that makes it really special – few other NNRs in the whole of Britain cover that range of habitats.

Left Sunrise blushes the quartzite summit of Liathach, seen from across Loch Clair

1

THE POISONED ISLE

During World War II, remote and uninhabited Gruinard Island in Gruinard Bay was the site of a biological warfare test of anthrax by British scientists from Porton Down.

Eighty sheep were taken to the 5-acre island, and bombs filled with anthrax spores were exploded close to where the sheep were tethered. The sheep quickly became infected and died within days of exposure. The scientists concluded that a large release of anthrax spores would render German cities uninhabitable for decades.

After the tests, visits to the island were obviously prohibited, except for periodic checks to determine the levels of contamination. In 1986, work started to decontaminate the island, and a formaldehyde solution was sprayed over it. A flock of sheep was then placed on the island and remained healthy. On 24 April 1990, after 48 years of quarantine, the warning signs were removed and the island was declared safe.

2

3

4

5

The semi-arctic quartzite plateau of the summit supports ground-hugging shrubs such as heather, crowberry, alpine bearberry and the pink-and-red-flowered mountain azalea. Rarities include the largest British population of the sharp-leaved prostrate juniper, and the bright orange-leaved liverwort *Herbertus borealis*, which is otherwise found only on three sites in Norway. This is the kingdom of true mountain birds like the ptarmigan, dotterel and snow bunting, and you may just get a glimpse of the mountain hare with its changing winter coat.

These magnificent mountains have equally wonderful stretches of water at their feet, such as Loch Maree, according to Murray one of the two 'most excellent' of Scotland's inland waters, and to fellow mountaineer Tom Weir, the embodiment of 'Highland grandeur'. Loch Torridon was reckoned by Alfred Wainwright, famous for his pictorial guides to the Lakeland fells, as 'the grandest prospect in Scotland'.

The shores of these beautiful lochs are often studded with rocky headlands and clothed by ancient, semi-natural woodlands of Scots pine, oak and birch. The coastline of the Wester Ross NSA is equally splendid, and around Loch Ewe, Loch Gairloch and Gruinard Bay, where sinister Gruinard Island (see box) is located, there is a pleasing mixture of beaches, islands, headlands and small, self-contained crofting settlements, such as Gairloch, Poolewe and Gruinard.

1 Gruinard Bay **2** Female wildcat **3** Mountain hare in her winter coat **4** A group of walkers survey the fearsome gash which splits the summit of Sgurr Mhor on Beinn Alligin **5** The red berries of mountain bearberry in the Beinn Eighe NNR

OTHER HIGHLAND NSAs

Extending 29 square miles (75sq km), the **Dornoch Firth** NSA represents the last undeveloped, fjord-like estuary on the east coast of Scotland. **Glen Strathfarrar** NSA covers 15 square miles (38sq km) of the steep-sided glen between the Culligran Falls and Loch Beannacharain. The tightly grained landscape of lochs, glens and hills of the **Knapdale** NSA covers 76 square miles (198sq km).

The **Kyles of Bute** NSA, 17 square miles (44sq km), consists of the curving straits that separate the Isle of Bute from the mainland, and includes Loch Riddon. Dominated by Ben Hope and Ben Loyal on the northern coast of Sutherland, the **Kyle of Tongue** NSA extends for 71 square miles (185sq km).

Watched over by the Glenfinnan Monument, erected in 1815 close to where Bonnie Prince Charlie gathered the clans in 1745 (see page 173), the **Loch Shiel** NSA encloses the sinuous sea loch and Glen Hurich in its 52 square miles (134sq km). **Loch Tummel** NSA covers 35 square miles (92sq km) of the former loch and now reservoir, running from the Pass of Killiecrankie to Tummel Bridge.

There are two NSAs around the Firth of Lorn, to the south and east of Mull on the west coast of Scotland. **Lynn of Lorn**, 19 square miles (48sq km), is centred on the flat, treeless island of Lismore, while the tiny **Scarba, Lunga and the Garvellachs** NSA covers just over 7 square miles (18sq km) and consists of the group of small islands at the entrance to the firth.

The isolated quartzite mountains of Foinaven, Arkle and Ben Stack watch over the majestic, lochan-strewn landscape of the 79 square mile (205sq km) **North West Sutherland** NSA. The **River Earn** NSA (Comrie to St Fillans) is a 12 square mile (30sq km) forest-dominated landscape on the Highland line at the eastern end of Loch Earn. Last, but not least, the **River Tay** NSA is a 22 square mile (56sq km) wooded area around the cathedral city of Dunkeld.

THE CUILLIN HILLS & TROTTERNISH, SKYE

The Cuillin Hills

The serrated ridge and abrasive gabbro rock of the Cuillin Hills of Skye are the nearest that Britain gets to the Alps, especially when they have a dusting of snow. And the whole of the 7-mile (11km) long main ridge is included in this 85 square mile (219sq km) National Scenic Area (NSA).

Centred on the remote and beautiful Loch Coruisk, vividly described by Sir Walter Scott in *The Lord of the Isles*, the NSA extends along Glen Brittle to the low, heath-covered sandstone Isle of Soay (Sheep Island) in Loch Scavaig, and east to the Red Cuillin Hills of Beinn na Caillich, Marsco and Glamaig to Loch Ainort.

There could hardly be a greater scenic contrast between the jagged gabbro peaks of the Black Cuillins, culminating in Sgurr Alasdair at 3,257ft (993m), and the smoothly rounded, pudding-basin shapes of the Red Cuillins. Both were created by volcanic activity during the Lower Tertiary period, about 60 million years ago, with the Black Cuillins of dark, basic gabbro forming first. Soon afterwards, there was an intrusion of acidic, granitic rock, richer in silica-based minerals, resulting in the Red Cuillins.

The Red Cuillins are often steep-sided and with isolated, conical peaks such as Marsco, Beinn Dearg and the reigning peak of Glamaig at 2,542ft (775m). Beinn na Caillich, which greets the visitor entering the area on the A87 at Broadford, means the Hill of the Witch in Gaelic. Loose scree smothers the summits, which are often scarred with deep gullies. Although they can appear red in certain light, they are more often described as reddish-brown or pink to grey in colour.

Rising straight from the sea, the Black Cuillins present some of the finest mountain profiles in Britain, and are famous throughout the world for both the severity of their rock climbing and the magnificence of their views. Seen from the hamlet of Sligachan, the range seems to be dominated by the shapely cone of Sgurr nan Gillean at 3,167ft (965m).

There are 14 Munros (see box, page 184) in the Cuillins. Defined as mountains of 3,000ft (914m) or higher, the Munros provide some of the most challenging climbing in Scotland. Most of them require some rock-climbing or scrambling skills, with only a few summits accessible by normal walking routes. At 3,046ft (928m), Bla Bheinn (or Blaven) is a magnificent Munro, consisting of slabs of naked

Right Clouds gather over the Cuillin Hills across a storm-tossed Loch Scavaig

BAGGING THE MUNROS

When Sir Hugh Munro (right), an original member and later president of the Scottish Mountaineering Club, first drew up a list of the 3,000ft high mountains of Scotland in 1891, he could have had little idea of what he was starting.

At the time, there were generally thought to be only about 30 such mountains in Scotland, but Munro's list included no fewer than 283. The craze now known as 'Munro bagging', to climb every one in your lifetime, began. The first man to achieve the magic total was the Reverend Archibald Robertson in 1901, and there are now over 4,500 Munroists who come from all walks of life and from all over Britain. The fastest time to complete the round is an astonishing 51 days; the slowest, by a 78-year-old man, took 64 years.

Many of the Munros, which now total 284 after some recalibration by the Ordnance Survey, are in very remote country.
The hardest to achieve is the so-called Inaccessible Pinnacle (nicknamed the In-Pinn) on the Cuillin Ridge, which is often wisely left till last. It was once memorably described by a Victorian visitor as having 'an overhanging and infinite drop on one side and a drop longer and steeper on the other'.

2

3

1

4

5

grey rock, isolated from the main ridge by Glen Sligachan, and best seen across Loch Slapin from the tiny whitewashed hamlet of Torrin.

The difficulty of crossing the 7-mile (11km) long Cuillin Ridge is reflected by the fact that it was not traversed in the summer until 1911, and much later in the winter. The ridge has airy crests, precipices, narrow sharp ridges with long drops, and massive buttresses, and requires a fair amount of scrambling. A rope and the knowledge of how to use it are essential to complete the formidable challenge provided by the Cuillin Ridge. Climbers love the excellent grip provided by the gabbro, but they must be aware of the futility of using a compass among the iron-rich rocks.

Glen Brittle to the west has some magnificent waterfalls, while Glen Sligachan leads from the famous climbers' base of the Sligachan Hotel at the head of Loch Sligachan, due north straight into the rocky heart of the Cuillins. The only major settlement is the tiny fishing village of Elgol, just outside the NSA on Loch Scavaig, which provides the classic view of the serrated ridges of the Black Cuillins to the north.

And at the very heart of these magnificent mountains lies Loch Coruisk, described by the travel writer H V Morton in *In Search of Scotland* (1929) as 'the grandest and most gloomy view in the British Isles'. Alfred, Lord Tennyson was not so lucky nor impressed during his visit, when he experienced typical Skye weather. He reported in his *Impressions of Scotland* (1848): 'Loch Coruisk, said to be the wildest scene in the Highlands, I failed in seeing. After a fatiguing expedition over the roughest ground on a wet day we arrived at the banks of the loch, and made acquaintance with the extremest tiptoes of the hills, all else being thick wool-white fog.'

The loch has also been the subject of many famous paintings by, among others, William Daniell (1769–1837), J M W Turner (1775–1851), Sidney Richard Percy (1821–86) and Alexander Francis Lydon (1836–1917).

Loch Coruisk is usually approached by boat from Elgol, or by experienced walkers only from Camasunary or Glen Brittle. The approach on foot along the coastline from Elgol involves negotiating the infamous Bad Step, where the crags of Sgurr na Stri sweep straight down into the icy waters of Loch Scavaig, and the 'path' involves a scramble across steep slabs.

1 View of Blaven from the Red Cuillins **2** Sir Hugh Munro, mountain-bagger extraordinaire **3** Waterfalls near Sligachan **4** Traditional heather-thatched croft at Luib **5** Painting of Loch Coruisk by William Daniell (1769–1837)

Trotternish

'The Quiraing is a nightmare of nature… (it) is frozen terror and superstition. This is a huge spire or cathedral of rock some thousand feet in height, with rocky spires or needles sticking out of it. Macbeth's weird sisters stand on the blasted heath, and Quiraing stands in a region as wild as itself. The country around is strange and abnormal, rising into rocky ridges here, like the spine of some huge animal, sinking into hollows there, with pools in the hollows – glimmering almost always through drifts of misty rain.'
From *A Summer in Skye* (1865) by Alexander Smith

The Trotternish peninsula in the northern part of Skye forms some of the most spectacular landslipped scenery in Britain, from the fantastical rocks of the Quiraing to the Sound of Raasay, and it is all included in this 19 square mile (50sq km) National Scenic Area (NSA).

Mountain photographer Walter Poucher, writing in his classic *The Magic of Skye* (1949), claimed: 'The weird rocks of the Quiraing make the most bizarre landscape in Britain.' Anyone who has walked through its amazing rock architecture to reach the oddly flat-topped Table will not disagree.

The landslipped basaltic rock towers and needles surrounding this smooth, grassy putting green under the cliffs of Meall nan Suireamach (1,781ft/543m) are among the most eccentric in Britain and said to be the result of the largest landslip of its kind in Europe. The black pinnacles culminate in the 100ft (30m) high sharply pointed Needle, the Prison and the Table. The highest points of this part of the tottering Trotternish Ridge are Bioda Buidhe at 1,522ft (464m) and Beinn Edra at 2,005ft (611m), from which there are stupendous views across the Sound of Raasay to Rona, Raasay and the coastline and peaks of Applecross on the mainland.

It was the deposition of Tertiary lava and igneous intrusions over older Jurassic sedimentary rocks, creating enormous pressure and instability, that led to these massive landslips, some of which are still occurring. The landslips also created steep, fissured cliffs of basalt at the higher levels, often with small, glittering lochans (small lochs) in the hollows beneath. Below these strange, other-worldly formations lie peat moors and the neat, white, Scandinavian-looking crofting settlements on the green and fertile shoreline of Staffin Bay. South of Staffin, the seaward side of the landslips forms cliffs of various heights, the most famous of which are the Kilt Rocks, where the waters of Loch Mealt drop straight into the sea in a spectacular, often rainbow-hued waterfall. The name Kilt Rocks comes from the fact that the basalt stands in vertical strands like the tartan of a Highlander's kilt.

The islands of Staffin and Eilean Flodigarry and Sgeir na Eireann are also included in the NSA, and the Quiraing and Beinn Edra form part of the Trotternish Ridge Site of Special Scientific Interest (SSSI).

1

2

3

1 The jagged basaltic pinnacles of the Old Man of Storr **2** A lone walker on the Table at the Quiraing, Trotternish **3** Waterfall at Kilt Rocks, northeast Skye **4** Sunrise over the weird landslipped rocks of the Quiraing

4

JURA

The distinctive triple cones of the Paps of Jura dominate the Inner Hebridean Isle of Jura, off Islay, and form the centrepiece of this 84 square mile (218sq km) National Scenic Area (NSA), which covers only the southern half of the island.

The domed tops of the Paps (meaning breasts) rise to nearly 2,300ft (over 700m) to the south of the deep sea loch of Loch Tarbert. The highest of the Paps is Beinn an Oir, meaning Hill of Gold, which rises to 2,575ft (785m), but the only gold you're likely to find there will be fool's gold, or iron pyrites. The other mountains in this compact little range are Beinn Shiantaidh at 2,483ft (757m) and Beinn a' Chaolais at 2,405ft (733m).

So distinctive are the Paps of Jura that they can be seen from the Isle of Man, the Antrim coast of Northern Ireland and many islands, peninsulas and mountains on the west coast of Scotland, including as far south as the Cobbler and Ben Lomond. They were also the subject of a famous 1902 painting by William McTaggart, now in the Kelvingrove Art Gallery, Glasgow.

Formed of ancient Dalradian quartzite rocks, the Paps rise abruptly from the rolling moorland of Jura forest, and their summits are crowned with extensive slopes of sparkling quartzite scree, which shimmer in the sun and are often mistaken for snow when viewed from afar.

The Scottish writer Alasdair Alpin MacGregor compared the Paps of Jura with the Cuillins of Skye for their steep-sided elegance, rising up straight from the coastal plain. Further south, the summit slopes of Glas Bheinn at 1,840ft (561m) and Brat Bheinn at 1,122ft (342m) are split by deep, western-flowing glens leading down to the Sound of Islay.

The western coastline of southern Jura has some of the finest raised beaches and cliffs in Scotland, seen to best effect at places like South Ebudes, a Site of Special Scientific Interest (SSSI), and Rubh' a' Chrois-aoinidh. These beaches, now well inland, were formed by a process known as isostatic uplift at a time when the sea level in the Sound of Islay was much higher than it is today, as the land rose at the end of the Ice Age. Some quartzite boulders are now found as high as 131ft (40m) above the sea, and there is also an impressive array of other relics from the days when the sea level was higher, including ancient sea caves and cliffs. The heavily indented bays and the islets, known as the Small Isles, on the sheltered eastern side of the island are generally less rugged and clothed in belts of woodland. The lighthouses of Skervuile and Na Cúiltean flash a warning to boats on this treacherous coast.

The island's population is only about 200, compared with an estimated red deer population of 5,500. Human settlement is centred on the east coast along the single-track A846 road. Within this area, near the village of Craighouse, is the township of Keils, famous for having retained its traditional run-rig strip fields and cruck buildings, in addition to being the home of the famous Isle of Jura whisky distillery.

There is a ferry from Port Askaig on Islay across the Sound of Islay to picturesque Feolin Ferry on the west coast of Jura. A road extends from Feolin Ferry around the southern half of the island to Tarbert and the other ferry terminus at Craighouse.

1 Evening light illuminates the Paps of Jura: Beinn a' Chaolais in the foreground, Beinn an Oir beyond **2** A wee dram at the Isle of Jura distillery **3** This isolated lodge on the shore of Loch Tarbert is accessible only by boat or a five-hour walk

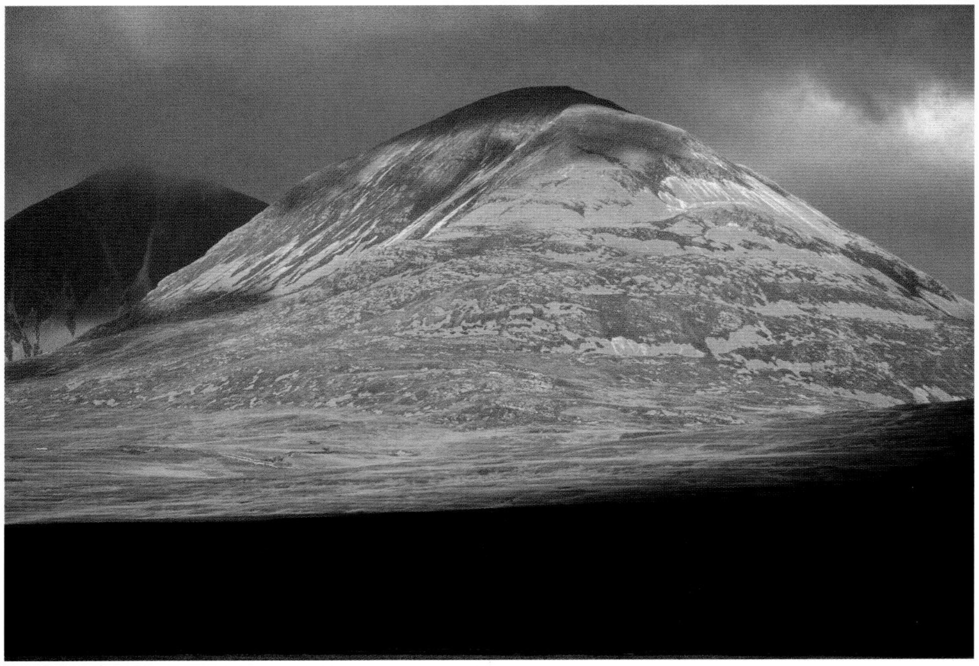

1

2

3

1

2

3

SOUTH LEWIS, HARRIS & NORTH UIST, & SOUTH UIST MACHAIR

The South Lewis, Harris and North Uist National Scenic Area (NSA) is one of the largest, covering 423 square miles (1,096sq km). It extends from Loch Róg on Lewis in the north and takes in the whole of the island of Harris, and North Uist as far south as Scolpaig and Loch Euphort. South Uist Machair is a quite separate NSA and much smaller at 24 square miles (61sq km). It comprises the coastal strip from Dreumasdal to the southern end of the island at Pol a'Charra.

Harris

Harris has the highest peaks in the Outer Hebrides, rising to 2,621ft (799m) at An Clisham. From its summit, the views extend from Cape Wrath in the north to the Cuillins of Skye and even as far as St Kilda, way out west in the Atlantic.

The glens of Harris are steep-sided and lined with precipitous crags – such as the enormous overhanging buttress of Sron Uladail at the northern end of the Oireabhal ridge – which give them the feel of much higher mountains. In the east, deep tidal sea lochs, such as Loch a Siar, with its large, peak-topped island of Taransay, and Lochs Reasort, Tamnabhaigh and Tealasbhaigh, penetrate deeply into the hills.

This deeply dissected cnoc-and-lochan (small hills and lakes) topography has numerous bays and islets, where isolated crofting communities fit unobtrusively into the environment. In contrast, the west coast of Harris comprises wide, sandy beaches, such as those around West Loch Tarbert and the Sound of Taransay, backed by flower-rich machair pastures (see box, page 192). The beautiful Sound of Harris is punctuated by the large islands of Pabbay and Berneray, which act as stepping stones and provide a visual link between South Harris and North Uist.

In 2009, the people of Harris voted more than two to one in favour of plans to make the entire island Scotland's third national park. They claimed that the designation would help to combat almost a century of chronic depopulation. The current population of Harris stands at around 1,800 people, and school rolls are steadily dropping. But in January 2011, the Scottish Government

4

1 The glorious white sandy beach at Seilebost, near Luskentyre, Harris **2** Interior of St Clement's church, Rodel, Harris **3** Brightly painted general stores in Tarbert, Harris **4** Patterned rocks on the beach at North Uist

THE MACHAIR

The machair coastal pastures that exist in places like South Uist are one of the rarest habitats in Europe, found only in the north and west of Britain and Ireland. Almost half of the Scottish machair occurs in the Outer Hebrides, with the best and most extensive in the Uists and on Barra.

Machair sand has a high shell content, sometimes as much as 80 or 90 per cent. The word *machair* is Gaelic, meaning an extensive, low-lying, fertile plain. It has now become a recognized scientific term for this kind of specific coastal feature, sometimes defined as a locally cultivated type of dune pasture (often calcareous), which has developed in wet and windy conditions.

The machair is farmed traditionally by the crofters of the isolated settlements of South Uist, who do not use any kind of artificial fertilizer. By August of each year, the crofters' sheep and cattle have grazed it to a uniform bright green.

announced that it would not consider a case for national park status for Harris in the current economic climate and without the full support of the Western Isles Council (Comhairle nan Eilean Siar). The Lewis-based council considered that, at this stage, a convincing case had not been made for a formal designation.

North Uist

The wide sandy straths (broad, flat river valleys) of North Uist provide a sharp contrast to the mountains of North Harris. Loch Maddy and Loch Euphort are deeply indented, island-studded sea lochs, which penetrate a low, hummocky, glaciated relief. These, in turn, are studded with lochans (small lochs) and dominated by the long ridge of Maireabhal, which rises to 755ft (230m).

South Lewis

The western flank of the island of Great Bernera in South Lewis marks the northern boundary of the NSA. To the south, it extends from the mountainous topography of South Lewis, including the summit of Beinn Mhor at 1,877ft (572m), out to the headland of Gob Rubh' Uisenis on the Sound of Shiant on the east coast.

The 1.5-mile (2.5km) long valley linking Loch Róg and Uig through Glen Bhaltos in the north of the NSA is nationally important for its glacial geomorphology. It is the most impressive meltwater channel in the Outer Hebrides, and part of a group of landforms that show evidence of how the last ice sheet from the Ice Age decayed some 18,000 to 14,000 years ago.

The road follows the impressive narrow gorge, which forms a distinct, separate corridor, cutting off all distant views of coast and sea, and offering a completely different experience from that found elsewhere within the NSA. The slopes of the steep-sided gorge are strewn with loose deposits of angular glacial debris, with large boulders and rocks at the base.

South Uist Machair

The outstanding physical characteristic of the South Uist Machair NSA is its low-lying, coastal machair pastureland (see box), a riot of colour in early summer with a dazzling profusion of up to 45 wildflower species per square metre. The machair lands of South Uist are never more than 2 miles (3km) wide at any point and are dotted with shallow, lime-rich lochans, which make up about a third of the surface area. As the great Scottish mountaineer and writer W H Murray wrote in *The Islands of Western Scotland: the Inner and Outer Hebrides* (1973): 'Until a man has seen a good machair… he may find it hard to realize that although the crofters call it "grass" it grows not grass but flowers.'

These low-lying pastures and water meadows are based on lime-rich sand, producing a flora unmatched in Britain. Buttercups, red and white clover, daisy, speedwell, dandelion, eyebright, bird's foot trefoil, harebell, thyme, yellow rattle, yellow and blue pansies and silverweed follow one another in seasonal splendour. Orchids are particular machair highlights, with both the rare pyramidal and fragrant varieties occurring in South Uist. There is a particular Hebridean type of spotted orchid, while a small stretch of the North Uist machair has its own variety of marsh orchid, *Dactylorhiza majalis scotica*, found nowhere else in the world.

The South Uist Machair NSA covers the western coast of South Uist, from Dreumasdal in the north to Pol a'Charra and the Sound of Eriskay in the south. The eastern limit is Uist's main road, the B888. Included in the NSA is the rocky headland of Rubha Aird a' Mhuile, which is a Site of Special Scientific Interest (SSSI), and part of the Loch Druidibeg National Nature Reserve (NNR).

1 White and red clover, lady's bedstraw and self-heal add a blaze of colour to the South Uist Machair **2** Peat cutting on North Uist **3** The illusive corncrake at Balranald, North Uist

2

3

LOCH NA KEAL, MULL

The view from Ben More on the island of Mull is one of the finest in the Inner Hebrides, and takes in the whole of the island-studded expanse of the 49 square mile (127sq km) Loch na Keal National Scenic Area (NSA).

The NSA extends northwest out to the distant, basaltic Treshnish Islands, with Bac Mór, Lunga and Fladda prominent. Closer at hand is the battleship-hull shape of the geologically famous island of Staffa, moored off Little Colonsay, Ulva and Gometra.

Loch na Keal is the principal sea loch on the west coast of Mull, and the NSA includes the shapely summit of Ben More and all the above-mentioned outlying islands, which can be seen from the summit. The loch is divided by the adjacent islands of Ulva and Gometra, with the northern half of the loch, known as Loch Tuath, running from Laggan Bay to Rubh' a' Chaoil.

The shapely peak of Ben More (Big Hill) is known to have been climbed as early as 1784 by William Thornton, an American, who was led by a local Campbell guide. The mountain, at 3,169ft (966m) and the only offshore Munro (a mountain over 3,000ft/914m, see box on page 184) not on Skye, presents a serious challenge to hillwalkers, especially if approached over the sharp eastern ridge.

West of Ben More, the southern boundary of the NSA extends along the north shore of the Ardmeanach peninsula to the outlying Criach Bheinn and the point of Rubha na h-Uamha, and the dramatically tiered landslip topography of the 1,000ft (305m) cliffs of Gribun, near Balnahard. Just offshore lies the small island of Inch Kenneth, with its ruined chapel and fine mansion house.

On the northern side, the NSA extends from Knock along the watershed between Meall nan Gobhar and Cruchan Loch Trath to the point of Rubh' a' Chaoil. The northern shore of Loch Tuath has a more intimate character. Its shoreline is indented with small bays into which hazel-, rowan- and alder-lined burns tumble, sometimes in waterfalls like that of Eas Fors, and a string of hamlets including Kellan, Lagganulva, Ballygown and Kilninian.

Eorsa is a green island with topography matching that of inner Loch na Keal, while the larger islands of Ulva, dominated by 1,027ft (313m) Beinn Chreagach, and Gometra have a shelved appearance. Most spectacular of these offshore islands is Staffa, which is one of the classic geological sites in the world. The great hexagonal basaltic columns of Fingal's Cave (see box), sweeping vertically up out of the sea, were formed by cooling lava during the Tertiary period around 60 million years ago.

1

2

1 Snow-capped Ben More (left) presents a serious challenge to hillwalkers **2** Juvenile common seal, Isle of Mull **3** The basalt columns of Fingal's Cave

A SYMPHONY IN STONE

The magnificent, cathedral-like cavern of Fingal's Cave on Staffa (left) was immortalized in music by the majestic cadences of Felix Mendelssohn's *Hebrides Overture*, composed after a rather uncomfortable visit to the island in 1829.

The 20-year-old German composer (1809–47) embarked with his friend Klingemann on the newly introduced paddle steamer from Oban to sail around the island of Mull, calling at Iona and Staffa. But it was a typically stormy day and all the passengers, including Mendelssohn, were very seasick.

However, the visit to Staffa and the unforgettable sight and sound of the enormous Atlantic swell surging into the pillared 227ft (69m) cavern obviously had a profound effect on him – he composed the popular overture immediately afterwards.

3

1

NORTH ARRAN

The Isle of Arran has often been described as the Highlands in miniature, and the more mountainous northern part of the island certainly has the feel of the Western Highlands, although it is only an hour's boat trip across the Firth of Clyde from Ardrossan on the mainland.

The north of Arran is dominated by serrated granite peaks, which culminate in Goat Fell, the 2,867ft (874m) centrepiece of the 92 square mile (238sq km) North Arran National Scenic Area (NSA). Ancient Highland rocks form the granite dome that is the basis of the spectacular scenery.

Dissected by deep and craggy glens such as Glen Rosa and Glen Iorsa, these rugged peaks rise to the crowning height of Goat Fell and the great rock fang of Cir Mhor at 2,618ft (798m). Other equally challenging summits include Caisteal Abhail at 2,818ft (859m) and Beinn Tarsuinn at 2,707ft (825m). These hills are a serious proposition to even experienced hillwalkers, but they are rewarded with outstanding views across to Bute, Cowal and Kintyre.

These magnificent hills are also the haunt of herds of red deer, while golden eagles and hen harriers can often be seen soaring on broad-fingered wings across the glens, where three unique species of Arran whitebeams are found on remote crags. The eastern part of the NSA is designated a Special Protection Area (SPA) mainly for its population of hen harriers.

The narrow coastal plain has typically Hebridean raised beaches, on which tiny clachan (hamlet) settlements have developed, many now in ruins after the infamous Highland Clearances of the 19th century. The only large settlements are the ferry port of Brodick, beneath Goat Fell on Brodick Bay, and Lochranza in the north, where there are the romantic, grey ruins of a 14th-century castellated tower house as well as a youth hostel.

One road – the A841 – encircles the island, sticking closely to the coastline, while the B880, the so-called String Road, threads through the glen of Machrie Water in the south of the NSA, between Brodick and Machrie Bay on the west coast. Here, there is much evidence of prehistoric activity, in the form of stone circles and standing stones.

Sheltered glens

The rich historical landscape of Arran was best described by the historian Robert McLellan in *The Isle of Arran* (1976): 'Everywhere in the upper glens are the ruins of old black-houses and turf dykes. In the straths or on the shores are the little oblong sites of ancient chapels. On the hilltops are faint traces of fortifications and on the moors, standing stones, stone circles and chambered cairns.'

The mild southern climate, warmed by the waters of the Gulf Stream, permits the growth of luxuriant vegetation in the sheltered glens. This is shown to dramatic effect in the famous rhododendron gardens of Brodick Castle, the Scottish baronial-style former seat of the Dukes of Hamilton, now in the hands of the National Trust for Scotland, and also the centrepiece of a popular country park.

Brodick Castle was originally a 13th-century fortified tower, which was developed by the Dukes of Hamilton during the 16th century. The present-day, largely Victorian extension was started by the 11th Duke in 1844. The walled garden, which dates from 1710, has been restored in the Victorian style, while the woodland garden, with its world-famous display of rhododendrons, was begun by the Duchess of Hamilton in 1923.

1 Looking towards Cir Mhor from Glen Rosa **2** Bronze Age stone circle on Machrie Moor **3** A hovering hen harrier

2

3

1

2

3

HOY & WEST MAINLAND, ORKNEY

The soaring cliffs and isolated sea stacks of the island of Hoy form a striking contrast with the more pastoral, archaeologically rich countryside of the West Mainland of Orkney in this 57 square mile (148sq km) National Scenic Area (NSA).

The ice-smoothed hills of northern Hoy dominate the West Mainland of Orkney, and the great cliffs and sea stacks of the western coast of the island create a lasting impression when seen from Dunnet Head, the most northerly point of the British mainland, on the Caithness coast.

Prominent in this view across the Pentland Firth, close to Rack Wick Bay, is the isolated, tottering sandstone sea stack of the Old Man of Hoy, 450ft (137m) high and unclimbed until 1966. A team comprising top climbers Chris Bonington, Rusty Baillie and Tom Patey took three days over its ascent.

The precipitous western coast of Hoy, south and west from Linksness in Hoy Sound, is split by vertical, wave-worn chasms known as geos, such as the Geo of Hellia and the Kame of Hoy, and isolated sea stacks including the Old Man of Hoy. The cliffs provide a home to numerous sea birds, and for this reason the west coast of Hoy is an RSPB reserve, providing an airy home for about 120,000 birds. These include nationally important populations of fulmar, great black-backed gull and guillemot.

This wild and windswept coastline reaches nearly 1,109ft (338m) at St John's Head to the north of the Old Man, while to the south lies Rora Head and another line of cliffs stretching to Sneuk Head. In the attractive glaciated valley of the South Burn, running from the village of Rackwick to Quoyness, stands the Dwarfie Stane (stone), a unique Neolithic rock-cut chambered tomb carved out of a huge block of sandstone. The name is said to be derived from local legend, which claims the dwarf Trollid lived there. Ironically, though, it has also been considered to be the work of giants.

To the north, across the South Burn, the rounded hills rise to 1,578ft (481m) at Ward Hill, which is a Site of Special Scientific Interest (SSSI) noted for its rare plant life, as well as Cuilags at 1,421ft (433m).

The town of Stromness, with its narrow, paved streets and quaint closes, climbs steeply from its harbour on the Orkney

1 Fishing boat leaving snow-covered Stromness harbour in winter **2** Little ringed plover nesting on Orkney **3** Seagulls flock around a fishing trawler, Orkney **4** The tottering sea stack of the Old Man of Hoy

4

1

2

3

mainland across the impressive tidal race of Hoy Sound. Here, the whale-shaped Graemsay Island compresses the waters of Clestrain Sound flowing in and out of Scapa Flow to the southwest.

Stromness dates back at least to Viking times, and its natural harbour and relatively calm waters have provided a welcome haven for generations of seafarers using the surrounding storm-tossed waters of the Atlantic Ocean and the North Sea. Orkney and its seaways have always been a strategic point for navigation, and in times of war, such as during the Napoleonic Wars and World Wars I and II, they have been used as an alternative route to the potentially dangerous English Channel. The town was also important to the former herring fishing industry. Its northerly position provided strong links to the Arctic, particularly through whaling, and it was used as a base for the Hudson Bay Company in opening up the wastes of northern Canada.

Prehistoric wonders

But Orkney is perhaps most famous for the wealth of its prehistoric remains. Near the Bridge of Waith, on the road to Kirkwall and at the end of the Loch of Harray, stands a group of some of the most impressive monuments in Europe. These make up the Heart of Orkney World Heritage Site, inscribed by UNESCO in 1999.

The great Neolithic chambered cairn of Maes Howe, 115ft (35m) across, covers the finest passage grave in Britain and is one of the wonders of the prehistoric world. As you stoop through the confined 36ft (11m) long entrance passage, it suddenly opens out into a tall, corbel-vaulted central chamber, which soars some 12.5ft (3.8m) above your head.

A large monolith stands at each corner of the chamber, while on both sides, regular rectangular openings give access to small side cells, which may have been used to inter the bones of the tomb's occupants. It has been estimated that the construction of Maes Howe, incorporating 30 tons of Orcadian sandstone, would have taken 100,000 man hours – an incredible feat of Neolithic organization and engineering.

Nearby, standing between the Lochs of Stenness and Harray, are the Ring of Brodgar and the Stenness stone circles, also dating from the New Stone Age. The 340ft (104m) wide Ring of Brodgar is the third largest stone circle in the British Isles. Covering an area of 90,793sq ft (8,435sq m), it stands on an eastward-sloping plateau on the Ness o' Brodgar – the thin strip of land separating the Harray and Stenness lochs.

The Ring of Brodgar is enclosed within a massive, 345ft (105m) diameter, rock-cut ditch with two entrance causeways. It originally consisted of about 60 standing stones, of which only 27 remain today. They are thought to have been erected some time between 2500 and 2000 BC.

The sheer scale of the four elegant, blade-like standing stones of Stenness, which reach a height of almost 20ft (6m), makes it one of the most striking of Orkney's many prehistoric monuments. Located on the southeastern shore of the Loch of Stenness, about a mile (1.6km) from the Ring of Brodgar, the Stones of Stenness were originally laid out around 3100 BC in the form of an ellipse.

Like its neighbour the Ring of Brodgar, the Stenness circle has been classed as a henge, as it was originally surrounded by a 144ft (44m) diameter rock-cut ditch. The henge had a single entrance causeway on the north side, outside which was a substantial earth bank, although little remains of this today.

You can get an unparalleled taste of what life was like on this windswept outpost of civilization over 4,000 years ago as you step into one of the eight surviving dwellings of the Neolithic village of Skara Brae. On the southern shore of the Bay of Skaill, just to the north of the NSA, Skara Brae is one of Orkney's most-visited sites and yet another of Orkney's remarkable prehistoric monuments.

The Neolithic buildings and their contents are incredibly well preserved due to the fact that they lay buried under sand until 1850, when a great winter storm exposed them. Not only are the walls of the houses still standing, and the low, covered alleyways between them still roofed with their original stone slabs, but the simple interior stone furnishings of each house provide a unique time capsule of what life was like in Neolithic Orkney.

1 The Ring of Brodgar, Orkney **2** An aerial view of Maes Howe, a Neolithic chambered cairn **3** Inside the Maes Howe tomb **4** Viking runic graffiti on the walls of Maes Howe **5** The exposed Neolithic village of Skara Brae

4

5

SHETLAND

Few maps of Britain show the Shetland Islands in their true position. Alongside the Orkney Islands, they are usually shown as an inset in the North Sea, tucked away in the top right-hand corner.

This is not surprising when you consider that the 100 islands that make up the Shetland archipelago are closer to the Arctic Circle than they are to London; closer to Bergen in Norway than they are to Aberdeen; and, at 60° north, on the same latitude as the southern tip of Greenland.

The Shetland National Scenic Area (NSA) covers 45 square miles (116sq km) and comprises seven coastal landscapes of outstanding scenic interest, principally in the southwest and northern extremities of this northernmost outpost of the British Isles. This fragmented NSA includes Hermaness, Foula, the southwest mainland, Eshaness, Fethaland, part of Muckle Roe and Fair Isle.

The scenic interest is predominantly coastal, with towering sandstone cliffs, geos (vertical, wave-worn chasms), natural arches, sea stacks, skerries (small, rocky islands) and fjord-like estuaries, known here by the Norse name of *voes*. According to Scottish Natural Heritage, Shetland has nearly 250 miles (400km) of cliffs, a fifth of Scotland's total.

1 A killer whale, or orca, breaches off Eshaness **2** The rocky coastline off the southern harbour on Fair Isle, with the wedge-shaped Sheep Rock in the background

1

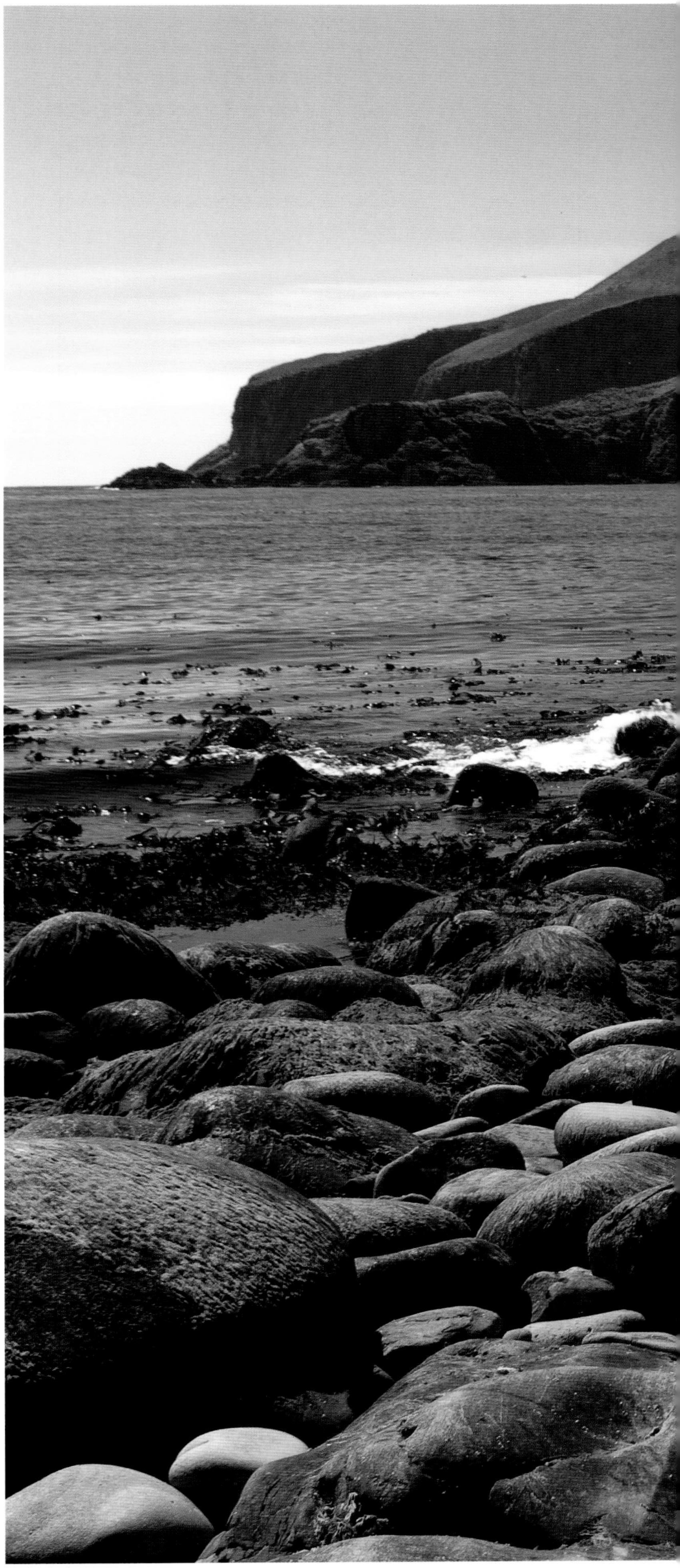

2

BIRDS OF FAIR ISLE

For such a small island, the sea bird population of Fair Isle is unequalled in Europe, and it is a prime location for spotting rare and unusual species of birds. The tiny island's total species list stands at over 360, but it was primarily for the sea birds, such as puffins, gannets (below right), guillemots and skuas, that most of the island was granted Special Protection Area (SPA) status in 1994.

Fair Isle became a haven for ornithologists in the 1930s, and one of the first to flock there was George Waterston (1911–80) of Edinburgh, who immediately fell in love with the island and began to make plans to open a bird observatory there. In 1947, Waterston, later to become director of the RSPB in Scotland, purchased the island. In the following year, the Fair Isle Bird Observatory was established in the old naval huts near North Haven.

Recently rebuilt at a cost of £4 million and re-opened in May 2010, the observatory has 20 commercial bedrooms and 10 reserved for researchers. Guests can go out on the cliffs with wardens ringing and recording puffins, and in the evening, after a home-cooked dinner, they are invited to join the staff for Bird Log, listing what they've seen, while enjoying more home baking and cocoa before retiring to bed.

2

3

1

4

Fair Isle

Said to be the most isolated inhabited island in Britain, Fair Isle lies midway between Orkney and the mainland of Shetland. Only 3 miles (4.8km) long and 1.5 miles (2.4km) wide, it is famous for its highly patterned knitwear, still made by a co-operative formed among the women of the island and now sold to passing cruise ships. It is also the home of one of the most important bird observatories in Europe (see box). The reigning 712ft (217m) summit of Ward Hill is littered with the unsightly remains of concrete military installations dating from World War II.

Fair Isle has a great diversity of cliffs, geos, sea stacks, skerries, natural arches, isthmuses and small bay-head beaches. Sheep Rock, with its vertical cliffs and smooth, sloping top, is a notable feature on the east coast near the observatory. Amazingly, it has about 10 acres of pasture on its sloping summit, and this was so valuable to the islanders that they used to climb it with chains, using ropes to raise and lower the sheep. Fair Isle is owned by the National Trust for Scotland.

Foula

Foula rises to 1,371ft (418m) at its highest point of Da Sneug, which overlooks the towering 1,200ft (366m) red sandstone cliffs of Kame on its northwestern coast. This dramatic island lies 18 miles (29km) to the west of the mainland of Shetland. Other notable geological features include sea stacks, skerries, caves and towering headlands, such as those at Waster Hoevda and Logat Head. The presence of large landslides along Foula's west coast indicates the unstable nature of the cliffs, as a result of failure along bedding planes in the sandstones. This is perhaps most dramatically displayed at Sneck ida Smaallie.

Shetland Mainland

The southwestern coastline of Shetland Mainland from Fitful Head (928ft/283m) in the south to the island-studded bay of the Deeps in the north, and the islands of East and West Burra and Tronda, with their distinctive and ancient run-rig settlement patterns, are also included in the NSA. (Run rig was a system of land tenure where each tenant was allocated detached 'rigs', or narrow strips of ploughed land, on a yearly basis.) The fjord-like indentations of Weisdale and Whiteness Voes in the north contrast strongly with the more open, cliff landscapes around the Loch of Spiggie and St Ninian's Isle, with its fine active tombolo (a sand spit linking it to the mainland) and ruined chapel in the south.

The 12th-century chapel on St Ninian's Isle is dedicated to Shetland's patron saint. In 1958, a local schoolboy found a hoard of beautiful 8th-century Celtic silver bowls and trinkets in a wooden box under a stone slab in the chapel grounds. It is thought

1 Northern cliffs of Fair Isle **2** Gannets engaged in a display ritual at the Hermaness National Nature Reserve **3** A fulmar rides the air currents above a Shetland sea cliff **4** 8th-century silver bowl found on St Ninian's Isle

that it may have been hidden during a Viking raid. Subsequent archaeological investigation discovered the remains of a pre-Norse chapel, which might indicate some kind of Culdee (early ascetic Christian) presence.

Muckle Roe and Eshaness

The western shore of Muckle Roe is made up of high, red sandstone cliffs bordering St Magnus Bay, while further north, across the bay, the rugged red granite headlands, cliffs, sea stacks and skerries of Eshaness are punctuated by the Sae Breck lighthouse and the Ness of Hillswick in the south. The name Eshaness comes, like so many Shetland names, from the Old Norse, *aesju nes*, meaning a headland of volcanic rock. Vertical volcanic cliff faces, like the descriptively named Grind of the Navir and a 820ft (250m) deep collapsed sea cave at the Holes of Scraada, characterize this wild and rugged coastline.

The village of Hillswick on Eshaness was developed in the 18th century as a deep-sea-fishing station by Thomas Gifford of Busta House, on the mainland, and there are the remains of an ancient broch (circular, dry-stone tower) on the shores of the Loch of Houlland.

The Drongs, between Eshaness and the Ness of Hillswick, are a series of thin, rocky pinnacles. Their appearance varies with the light, and on a misty night they can often be mistaken for ships under full sail. The Drongs include a high rock pillar, known as Slender Drong; the taller Main Drong; and two smaller stacks, Slim Drong and Stumpy Drong. They were drawn by David Henry Parry (1793–1826) to illustrate Samuel Hibbert's *Description of the Shetland Islands* published in 1822, and memorably engraved by Thomson of Edinburgh.

Fethaland

Further north on the mainland, the northern end of the North Roe peninsula is included in the NSA between Fugla Ness, Uyea Island and up to the Point of Fethaland and the outlying pinnacles of the Ramna Stacks. The former fishing lodges on Fethaland are evidence of what was once the largest fishing station in the Shetlands – up to 60 boats operated out as far as 50 miles (80km) west to the Far Haaf, on the very edge of the continental shelf. The single-storey lodges were lived in by the fishermen in season, while the former two-storey buildings, known as *böds*, combined a shop, housing for the beach master, and a store for fish.

Hermaness

Hermaness and the Burra Firth at the northern end of the island of Unst constitute the final frontier of this most remote NSA, with the sea stacks of lighthouse-crowned Muckle Flugga and the pinnacle of Out Stack taking the prize for the most northerly outposts of the British Isles.

The first lighthouse on Muckle Flugga was built in 1854, and the Scottish author Robert Louis Stevenson (1850–94) visited the present building (completed in 1858) in 1869, with his father Thomas Stevenson, who was then the construction engineer to the Board of Trade. Some people believe that the island of Unst influenced Robert in the writing of his classic adventure tale of pirates and buried gold, *Treasure Island*, published in 1883. Muckle Flugga lighthouse was finally automated in March 1995.

The eastern edge of Hermaness contains the most northerly military installations in the British Isles, with the rather ugly and obtrusive radar station on the 935ft (285m) summit of Saxa Vord.

1 Muckle Flugga and its lighthouse, which was built by the Stevenson family in 1854 **2** The Drongs sea stacks from the cliffs of the Neap, Eshaness **3** A grey seal bull tucks into a freshly caught cod

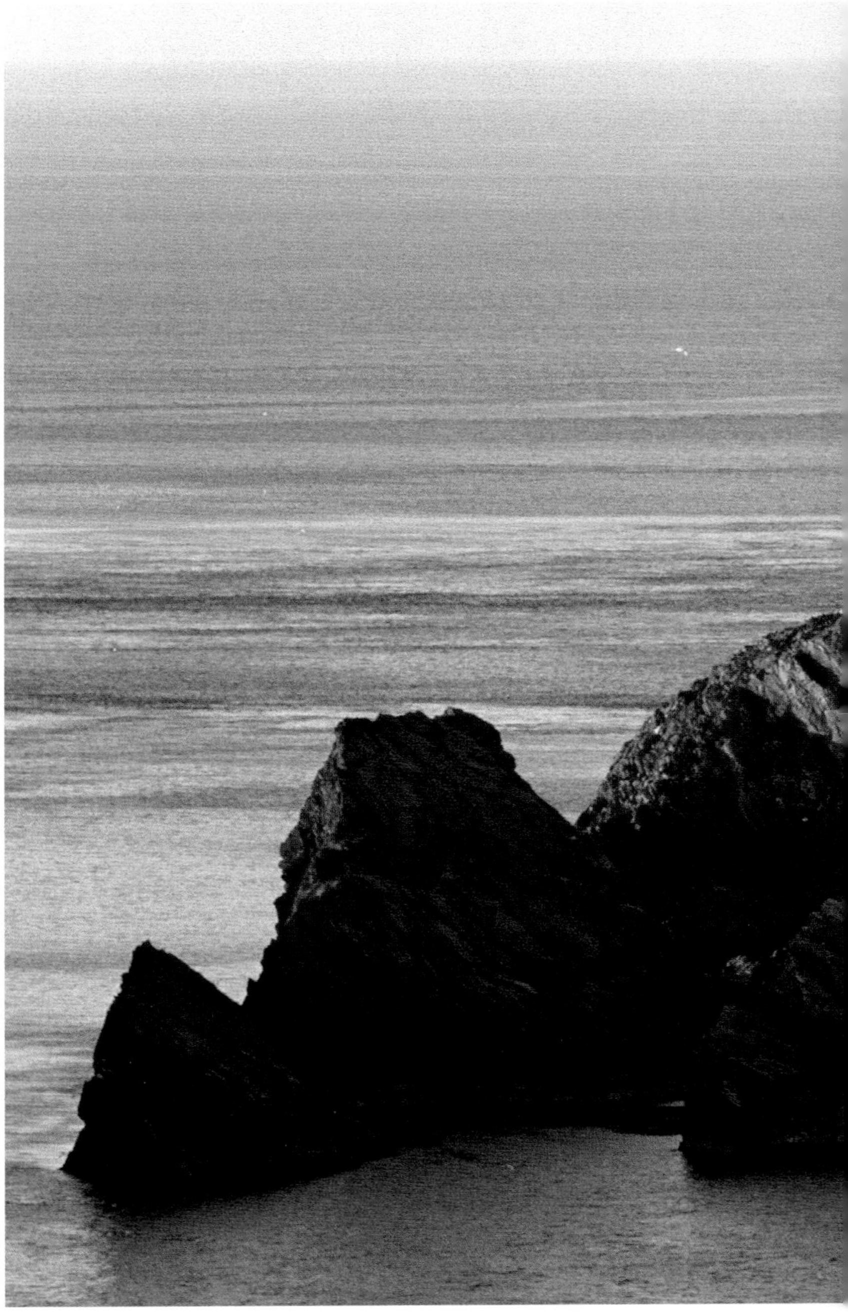

1

2

3

OTHER ISLAND NSAs

There is one other NSA in the Scottish Islands and that is the remote and windswept **St Kilda** archipelago, designated a World Heritage Site for both its natural and cultural significance. Situated about 40 miles (64km) due west of Benbecula in Scotland's Outer Hebrides, St Kilda consists of four main islands covering about 3.5 square miles (9sq km), with precipitous sea stacks and the highest sea cliffs in Britain.

THE SMALL ISLES

The compact group of Inner Hebridean islands comprising Rum, Eigg, Muck and Canna off the southwestern shores of Skye are known collectively as the Small Isles.

Each of the Small Isles has its own, quite different character but all have a distinctive Hebridean feel to them, and they form a fascinating, self-contained archipelago. Together they make up this spectacularly beautiful 60 square mile (155sq km) National Scenic Area (NSA).

Rum

Rum is a mountainous island, containing every element of the Hebrides. This includes the stepped country of Torridonian sandstones in the north around Kilmory Glen, the grassy terraces separated by cliffs of basaltic lava below the peak of Orval (1,873ft/571m) in the west, and the knife-edged gabbro ridges of the highest ground of the twin peaks of Askival at 2,661ft (811m) and Ainshval at 2,552ft (778m), also known as the Rum Cuillins, in the south. Sgurr nan Gillean (Peak of the Gullies), a southern outlier of Ainshval, even shares the name of the reigning northern Cuillin peak on Skye.

The distinctive Rum peaks were almost certainly named by Viking raiders as they sailed through the Hebrides, because most of their names are of Norse origin. Askival means 'the hill of the spear' and Ainshval 'the rocky ridge hill' – the 'val' suffix comes from the Old Norse *fjall*, meaning mountain.

Massive granite cliffs mark Bloodstone Hill, while Glen Dibidil is a textbook U-shaped glaciated valley. The only settlement of any size on Rum is the little township of Kinloch at the head of Loch Scresort on the east coast. Here, Kinloch Castle, with its walled garden, pasture and extensive areas of new, native and planted woodland, dominates Kinloch Glen.

The island formerly had a population of around 350, but the crofters were evicted from the land in 1826 – most of them ended up in Canada – when the laird, Alexander Maclean, cleared the island for sheep. But the sheep were not as profitable as Maclean had hoped, and by 1845 the island had been turned into a shooting estate by the Marquis of Salisbury, who had bought the island and introduced Rum's famous herd of red deer.

The island was then bought by John Bullough, a Lancashire industrialist, in 1887, and continued to be used as a deer-stalking estate, with the public firmly excluded. John's son George inherited the island in 1897 and built the crenellated red sandstone Kinloch Castle, which still stands as a decaying monument to Edwardian

Left Sunset over the Isle of Rum

elegance. The servants' quarters at the rear of the castle are now used as a hostel and bistro by Scottish Natural Heritage, and there are plans to reopen the rest of the castle after an extensive programme of refurbishment. George Bullough also built the somewhat pretentious, classical Greek temple-style mausoleum for the family graves in lonely Glen Harris.

Most of Rum consists of large tracts of moorland and mountain, and the whole of the island was designated a National Nature Reserve (NNR) when it was sold to the Nature Conservancy Council in 1957. Apart from the red deer, Rum is perhaps most famous for being the place where white-tailed sea eagles were reintroduced from Norway in 1975. After a slow start, these magnificent birds have spread to other parts of the Hebrides, and they share the Rum skies with a good population of native golden eagles.

The social future for Rum looks brighter today, as crofting was reintroduced to Kinloch Glen in 2009 by the Rum Community Trust. And, in March 2010, the Trust celebrated the acquisition of Kinloch village, after many years of trying to secure land for housing and other local enterprises.

Eigg

The Sound of Rum separates Rum from Eigg, which is formed mainly from volcanic basalts and is, therefore, much more fertile than its larger neighbour. A steep-sided ridge of Jurassic sandstone forms impressive cliffs in the north of the island, while the southern end is dominated by the imposing Sgurr of Eigg (1,293ft/394m), a block of volcanic pitchstone lava that forms a long, undulating ridge of bare grey rock. Viewed end-on from the sea, it forms a tremendous vertically walled, flat-topped tower, while a series of large caves punctuates the rest of the coastline.

Eigg is an island of small crofts with rich grazing pastures and meadows (especially around Cleadale), deciduous woodlands, young conifer plantations and some exotic garden planting around the Victorian lodge and in Galmisdale. There are large areas of rough moorland to the southwest and to the north. The Isle of Eigg Heritage Trust was set up in 1997 to secure the island's future and to provide its small population of under 70 with the opportunity to grow through its own sustainable initiatives.

Muck

Most of the 30-strong population of the low-lying island of Muck, off the southwestern coast of Eigg, live in Port Mór on the southeast coast. The areas around the summit of Beinn Airein at 453ft (138m) and the islet of Eilean nan Each remain uninhabited. Muck is formed of Tertiary basalt, which gives it that familiar stepped profile, and the rock has been worn into a series of cliffs and caves around the coast. Inland, fertile green pastures rise to the summit of Beinn Airein in the west.

Canna

At the northern end of the Small Isles archipelago is Canna, another basaltic island but with inland cliffs above its grassy slopes and a spectacular northern coastline of caves, arches and sea stacks. Compass Hill on Canna contains large deposits of iron that can sometimes affect sailors' compasses.

As you approach the lower island of Sanday, linked by a bridge to Canna, St Edward's Catholic church, built for visiting herring fishermen but no longer used for worship, commands a prominent position overlooking the harbour. MacCulloch's 'rude' peaks of Rum provide a beautiful backdrop.

1 A view of Rum from Laig Bay, Isle of Eigg **2** A lone boat moored on Canna Island
3 The precipitous Sgurr of Eigg (An Sgurr) dwarfs the crofter's cottage at its foot

1

2

3

EILDON & LEADERFOOT

The distinctive triple summits of the Eildon Hills dominate the 14 square mile (36sq km) Eildon and Leaderfoot National Scenic Area (NSA), which is based around the confluence of the River Tweed with the Leader Water. Centred on the town of Melrose, with its ancient Mercat (market) Cross and the romantic ruins of a 12th-century, red sandstone Cistercian abbey, most of the NSA lies in the shadow of the Eildon Hills, which form such a distinctive feature of many Border views.

The Eildons, formed by volcanic action around 350 million years ago, stand out as a heather- and rough grass-covered island in a sea of rich lowland farming country, generally known as 'Scott Country'. The area was much loved by Sir Walter Scott (1771–1832), who lived in feudal splendour at nearby Abbotsford. Scott often featured the surrounding landscapes in his writing, for example in the poem *The Eve of St John*: 'Where fair Tweed flows round holy Melrose, And Eildon slopes to the plain…'

This sickly son of an Edinburgh lawyer, who became one of the most popular Victorian poets and novelists, fell in love with the countryside around Melrose after youthful visits to relatives in the Tweed Valley when he was suffering from childhood polio. Following his huge literary success, Scott bought a small farm 3 miles (5km) west of Melrose within sight of his beloved Eildons and, over the next dozen years, created the vast, many-towered, crenellated Gothic mansion of Abbotsford.

The highest summit of the Eildons is Eildon Mid Hill at 1,385ft (422m), with Eildon Western Hill just across a grassy saddle. But the most strategically placed is Eildon Hill North at 1,322ft (403m), which is topped by a monument to Scott and ringed by the embankments of a massive 40-acre Iron Age hillfort built by the native tribe of the Selgovae.

When the Romans captured the site in AD 79, they built a wooden signal station inside an enclosure on the summit to watch over their camp, known as Trimontium (Three Hills), which was just over a mile (1.6km) below to the northwest. Across the Leader Water, Black Hill at 1,030ft (314m) and White Hill at 712ft (217m) echo the geology, shape and character of the Eildons.

The whole scene is best appreciated from Scott's famous viewpoint near Bemersyde Hill, above the elegant 12th-century ruins of Dryburgh Abbey, built in a loop of the River Tweed, where the poet is buried. This is a well-wooded and fertile landscape of rich farms, where a sense of history seems to pervade every view.

Left Scott's view of the triple tops of the Eildon Hills

THOMAS THE RHYMER

The ballad of *Thomas the Rhymer*, which dates back at least to the 13th century, is closely connected with the area of the Eildon Hills. Several different versions of the ballad exist, but most tell how Thomas met with the Queen of Elfland on the hills and either kissed or slept with her and was transported to Fairyland. The Eildon Tree Stone, a large moss-covered boulder on the road 2 miles (3km) west of Melrose, is said to mark the spot where the Fairy Queen led Thomas into the heart of the hills.

Thomas stayed in the Fairy Queen's castle until she told him it was time to return to his homeland. He asked for a token to remember her by, and she offered him the choice of becoming either a harpist or a prophet, and he chose the latter. After a number of years spent prophesying, Thomas bade farewell to his homeland and, presumably, returned to Fairyland, from where he has not yet returned.

Rhymer's Glen was created by Sir Walter Scott at his home in Abbotsford, just outside the NSA. The symbol of the Eildon Tree has persisted as inspiration for Scottish poetry and song, through the work of Sydney Goodsir Smith and *The Eildon Tree* poetry magazine.

Between its confluence with the Ettrick and that of the Teviot, the valley of the Tweed is wide, open and fertile, affording fine views. The surrounding shapely hills enclose the winding, wooded course of the river, and the main land uses are arable, pasture, plantation and moorland. The settlement pattern is closely related to the physical geography of the area, creating a very human and cultivated landscape.

It is not surprising that Scott found inspiration for his work here. He once wrote: 'I can stand on the Eildon Hill and point out forty-three places famous in war and verse.' Most famous among these is probably the medieval ballad of Thomas the Rhymer (see box), and it is claimed that the last resting place of the legendary King Arthur lies hidden in a cave beneath the Eildon Hills.

The Romantic painter J M W Turner (1775–1851) visited Scott at his home in Abbotsford in 1831 and his works also highlight the timelessness of the landscape. These include *View of the Tweed with Melrose and the Eildon Hills* and *A View of the River Tweed and Dryburgh Abbey*.

Between 1750 and 1850, there were no fewer than 300 editions of the famous poem *The Seasons* by local man James Thomson. It has been claimed that no single British poet contributed more to awakening the appreciation of the natural world than Thomson. Probably best known for writing the lyrics of *Rule Britannia*, Thomson (1700–48) was born in Ednam, Roxburghshire, and is commemorated by the classical Temple of the Muses, erected by the 11th Earl of Buchan in 1817 on Bass Hill on the banks of the Tweed, near Dryburgh. Robert Burns wrote a special poem, *Address to the Shade of Thomson,* for the opening of the temple.

Weaving and bleaching

Most of the towns and villages in the NSA developed as part of the tweed and knitwear industry, which brought wealth to the Scottish Borders, utilizing the distinctive, Roman-nosed Cheviot Hill sheep and the availability of water power for the looms. Chief among these towns is Melrose, where linen weaving and bleaching have given the name Bleachfield to an area to the west of the town. The impressive remains of a large, water-powered textile mill still exist at Leaderfast.

The great Cistercian abbey of St Mary at Melrose served the church and the state of Scotland for four centuries, from its foundation in 1136 to its dissolution in about 1556. The town of Melrose, founded to serve the abbey, grew up at its southern gate. The heart of the 14th-century Scottish resistance leader Robert the Bruce is allegedly buried within the precincts of the abbey. Another great resistance leader, Sir William Wallace, is remembered in the giant, 21ft (6.4m) high red sandstone statue that stands in the grounds of Bemersyde House, near Dryburgh.

1 Looking over the rooftops of Melrose from the ruins of the abbey **2** River Tweed at Dryburgh **3** Statue of William Wallace near Dryburgh **4** The ruined medieval architecture of Dryburgh Abbey

2

3

4

EAST STEWARTRY COAST, NITH ESTUARY & FLEET VALLEY

The wide tidal mudflats of Mersehead Sands on the northern shore of the Solway Firth shelter the 17 square mile (45sq km) East Stewartry Coast National Scenic Area (NSA), one of the smallest of the Scottish NSAs. The almost adjacent Nith Estuary NSA, covering 55 square miles (142sq km) is where the River Nith and Lochar Water flow into the Solway.

The slightly larger 20 square mile (53sq km) Fleet Valley NSA just down the coast to the west is centred on the estuary of Fleet Bay, where the Big Water of Fleet feeds into Wigtown Bay.

East Stewartry Coast

This NSA is centred on Rough Firth, and Orchardton and Auchencairn Bays. West of Southerness Point, the broad tidal flats of the Mersehead Sands mark the point where the saltings of Preston Merse meet the fossil cliffs and raised beaches of the rocky Sandyhills Coast. Sandyhills Bay, with its dunes and sheltering woodlands, is separated from Mersehead Sands by the meandering intertidal stretch of Southwick Water. Inland, the hills of Dalbeattie Forest are partly wooded and moorland, rising to over 984ft (300m) at Maidenpap and Long Fell.

To the west, the hills become more wooded as they enclose Rough Firth, and Orchardton and Auchencairn Bays, which are divided by the wooded promontories of Almorness Point and Ton Point. Heston Island and Rough Island, in the hands of the National Trust for Scotland, provide important sanctuaries for the abundant birdlife of the estuary.

The NSA is enclosed to the west by the ridge of hills running from Balcarry Point to the 1,282ft (391m) summit of Bengairn Hill, crossing the summits of Screel Hill and Croach Hill to reach the River Urr. Dalbeattie, noted for its granite quarries, is the natural centre for the region but it lies north of the NSA, at the first crossing of the River Urr.

The only settlements within the NSA are Kippford, a yachting centre on Rough Firth, and, to the south, the quiet seaside resort of Rockcliffe. Nearby is the Mote of Mark, the remains of a prehistoric vitrified fort (see box), now cared for by the National

1

1 View of Kippford and the River Urr from near Palnackie **2** Barnacle geese rise from the Mersehead RSPB Reserve **3** Dalbeattie Forest

VITRIFIED FORTS

A vitrified (that is, turned to glass) fort is the name given to stone hilltop enclosures, generally dating back to the Iron Age, whose walls have been subjected to intense heat.

All of these dry-stone structures (there are about 50 throughout Scotland) seem to have been consolidated by the fusion of the rocks from which they were built. In many instances, the pieces of rock are enveloped in a glassy, enamel-like coating, which binds them into a whole, and sometimes the entire length of the wall presents a solid mass of vitreous material.

Archaeologists disagree about why and how the walls were subjected to vitrification. Some claim that it was done to strengthen the walls, but this is unlikely because heating actually weakens the structure of the stone. Battle damage is also unlikely to be the cause, as the walls must have been subjected to carefully maintained fires over a long period for vitrification to take place.

The latest theory is that the forts may have been deliberately burned down in some kind of ritual ceremony, as seems to have happened at Navan in County Armagh, Northern Ireland.

2

3

Trust for Scotland. Overlooking the Urr estuary, this defended hilltop was occupied during the 6th century and appears to have been destroyed by fire in the 7th. Archaeological research has determined that the top of the hill was enclosed by a massive stone and timber-laced rampart, which was apparently affected by fire, and that inside there was a timber hall surrounded by workshops and stables.

This was evidently a wealthy site with trading contacts across Europe, and was possibly the court or citadel of a powerful Dark Age chieftain. Finds from the site include glass beads and wine jars from central France and glassware from Germany. Elegant bronze jewellery in a distinctive Celtic style, obviously made by local craftsmen, has also been discovered. The tumbled remains of the ramparts can still be seen and an on-site interpretation panel has a vivid reconstruction of the fort.

Nith estuary

The estuary of the Nith is dominated by the shapely granite cone of Criffel. This 1,867ft (569m) hill is a particularly prominent feature on the horizon when seen rising from the coastal plains from across the Solway Firth in Cumbria or from the northern fells of the Lake District.

At the foot of Criffel, near Kirkconnell, are the romantic, red sandstone ruins of Sweetheart Abbey (Historic Scotland), a 13th-century Cistercian abbey, where the embalmed heart of John Balliol (d.1268) – a local landowner by marriage and founder of Balliol College, Oxford – lies buried in a casket of ivory and silver.

On the opposite (eastern) bank of the Nith estuary stands the imposing Caerlaverock Castle (also Historic Scotland), the epitome of a medieval stronghold, with its unique, triangular plan, moat, twin-towered gatehouse and imposing battlements. Caerlaverock

1

2

3

was founded in the late 13th century by the Maxwell family, and withstood several sieges by the invading English before it was finally subdued by Protestant forces in 1640.

The castle is within the Caerlaverock National Nature Reserve (NNR), and the nearby 2.2 square mile (6sq km) Wildfowl & Wetlands Trust nature reserve at Eastpark Farm is a great place to watch the wildfowl that flock to overwinter here. These include almost the entire Svalbard (Spitsbergen) population of barnacle geese, with many of the birds staying for all or part of the winter. The reserve has enabled the population of these handsome geese to recover from just 500 birds in the 1940s to over 25,000 today.

Fleet Valley

Fleet Bay, with its guardian Islands of Fleet, is dominated by the 1,500ft (456m) hill mass of Cairnharrow, to the west of the estuary, with its twin outliers of Ben John and Mill Knock. The relief is not so pronounced on the western side of the bay, where the well-wooded Bar Hill rises just south of Gatehouse of Fleet, the only major settlement in the area.

The NSA runs inland as far as the southern end of the Rig of Drumruck and the foothills of the 2,330ft (710m) Cairnsmore of Fleet. The landscape of the Fleet Valley NSA is one of rich, well-managed mixed farms, with a wealth of broadleaved woodlands clothing the valley sides and evidence everywhere of the area's past history.

The Murray Islands, four small uninhabited islands off Carrick Point in the Islands of Fleet at the mouth of Fleet Bay, were gifted to the National Trust for Scotland by Mrs Murray Usher of Cally House, Gatehouse of Fleet, in 1991.

Gatehouse of Fleet is the focal point of the valley of the Fleet Water and has connections with both Sir Walter Scott and Robert Burns. Scott called the town Kippletringan in his popular novel *Guy Mannering*, published anonymously in 1815, while Burns is said to have composed *Scots wha hae* during a drunken night at the Murray Arms Hotel.

The town has existed since the mid-18th century, when the entrepreneur James Murray decided to build his summer home Cally (now a hotel) there in 1765. Over the next century, the town developed into a centre for industry, particularly for cotton mills. The inventor of clockwork mechanisms, Robert Williamson, also set up a workshop in the town in 1778 but it burned to the ground and, tragically, claimed his life in 1794.

Gatehouse of Fleet was also the birthplace of the popular Victorian artist John Faed (1819–1902). He conceived a number of projects in the town, including the clock tower and the town hall, which was opened in August 1885 by his brother Thomas.

A mile (1.6km) to the southwest of Gatehouse of Fleet on a rocky cliff overlooking Fleet Bay are the well-preserved remains of the six-storey, late 15th-century tower house Cardoness Castle. Now in the hands of Historic Scotland, the castle was originally owned by the McCulloch family of Galloway, also known as the McCullochs of Myreton. They abandoned it in the late 17th century, following the execution of Sir Godfrey McCulloch for the murder of a Clan Gordon neighbour.

OTHER SOUTHERN UPLANDS NSAs

The other NSA in the Scottish Lowlands is **Upper Tweedale**, a narrow, steep-sided valley flanked by rounded hills between Broughton and Peebles, which covers 40 square miles (105sq km).

1 Sandgreen on Fleet Bay **2** Kirkcudbright Pipe Band leading the torchlight parade at the Gatehouse of Fleet gala **3** Anworth Church Millennium Memorial at Vinniehill above Gatehouse of Fleet

INDEX

Page numbers in *italic* refer to the illustrations